PASS THE BALL!

THE JOURNEY AND IMPACT AFTER THE SUICIDE OF WADE DEVIN MULLIGAN-ADAMS

A book written by

VENESSA ADAMS

Trafford rev. 12/22/2014

 www.trafford.com

North America & international
toll-free: 1 888 232 4444 (USA & Canada)
fax: 812 355 4082

When stepping into 'The Book,' pray faithfully

DEDICATION

This book is dedicated to my son, my reflection.

You taught me humbleness and unconditional love in such a short time. You were a true gift from God, a shining star that will light up our lives for a life time.

EST. 1995

CONTENTS

INTRODUCTION

So here I am, writing about the journey that a grandparent, a mother, a father, a brother or sister, an aunt or uncle, a cousin, a nephew or niece or a friend has to walk, after a choice of suicide has been made.

God has given me great insight into my son's life and what it would have entailed. Although painful, I know that I have to trust God in all things and that through His grace I will find peace on this earth.

The road that has been set out for me and my family is an awesome, but extremely hard road for any one person to follow. But God does not bring you or take you to a place, where He knows you will not be able to cope or deal with it.

His outstretched hand has held me steadfast in this walk, and when I decide to take a detour, I feel how that hand steers me back into alignment.

'A TRUE STORY OF A MOTHER'S HEART RENDERING JOURNEY'

And as I start writing, I'm peeling my heart open layer by layer.

This is how my story starts . . .

We are an average family, and I have accepted God into my life. And on accepting Him, I told God that I was aware that my children are borrowed to me and that I would give them back to Him to do His will. And that my most fervent prayer, is that they would follow in Jesus footsteps and choose the life of our SAVIOUR.

We battle financially but we have never really been short of anything. I always knew that God's hand was over me and my family, but not for one moment did I think that when I prayed and said to God, that I would stand firm in His word, I would not quiver or shake, but would be solid as rock for Him, that He would take me up on my offer, and that I would be tested far beyond any of my expectations.

So here goes . . .

Oh, Just a little message for my family and everyone who has gone through a suicide.

I am aware that reading this book will open a lot of wounds, but through this, I hope that we will find peace in the process. Perhaps this will make a lot of children and parents realize what the 'IMPACT OF A SUICIDE' leaves behind . . .

CHAPTER 1

THE BEGINNING OF OUR JOURNEY

Wade got sick a few days before Easter in 2010, he developed the flu. On Easter Saturday, he got up, said he was feeling much better and wanted to visit his uncle Jon. He said that he missed him and most especially wanted to watch the Arsenal game. He called his uncle Jon and then got up to go to the toilet where he collapsed. When Demi his sister lifted his head, he was soaked with perspiration, his entire body was wet. I called my brother Jonathan to tell him what had just happened, and that I was rushing him to hospital. Demi lifted her brother, and as heavy as Wade was, she carried him to the car, and climbed in with him in her hands. We drove to hospital, hazards on and driving like Michael Schumacher.

Our life was about to take a drastic change forever. At the hospital, they rushed him into the Trauma Section and started with a thorough examination on him but could not find anything that caused this. They came over to me to find out what medication I had given Wade. I had to contact Wade's weekend parents Clint and Deidre, because Wade had gotten sick while staying with them for a few days. I told the doctors what they had given Wade, but according to them, it could not have caused any damage.

Doctors are busy, in and out, but allow me to stay inside. I watch in amazement how all doctors in the trauma unit are pulling their weight. X-rays, scans, and instruments I never knew existed came to the fore, and I watched how one test after another was carried out on my son. I leave the room to inform my family about Wade. I look at them, the shock on their faces; it's a picture in my mind that will never leave me . . .

GOD'S HAND AT WORK

Eventually, after all the tests they could not pick up anything, and then called in a top surgeon to have a look at Wade, and he too, could not draw any conclusions.

In the meantime other family members had arrived and were waiting outside, some are in the waiting room, Jonathan, Wade's uncle, and his sister Demi are outside the trauma room. After the initial tests, the doctor called me and questioned me about Wade. The Surgeon that had been called in was convinced that Wade had overdosed. I was immediately upset and went again outside to inform Jonathan and Demi, and I can still remember as clear as daylight how upset they were because of what the doctor had to say.

Now if you knew Wade, then you would understand why they felt that way. I immediately set the record straight, and let them know that under no circumstances, did my son at any time do drugs, or even intended on doing in this life time. He was against anything that was not good for the body or the mind. He was a total health fanatic.

Let me tell you a bit about Wade . . .

BABY WADE

From the tender age of two Wade was already set in mind of what he was going to be when he grew up. From the age of six months Wade's ball went everywhere with him. It even slept with us, bathed with us and visited with us. Before he could walk, Wade held a ball at his side and that is where it stayed. The ball became a part of our lives. So when at two and half years of age, he begged his granddad to let him play for his granddad's under eight soccer team, Jonathan and Dad had no say in the matter, and on that Winter Saturday morning in 1997, Wade was registered with Bosmont Football Association, playing under eight for Goretti Football Club.

WADE'S LIFE

I often wondered, in my quiet moments, and I would question God silently within as to why He never gave me a son. Had God heard my questions and answered me by allowing Wade to come into my life? The bond that was formed was a bond entwined, no separation was possible, and through that our amazing journey started . . .

The day Wadey was born, I looked at this little boy and knew right then, that he was going to be special. And that I was going to have a relationship second to none with this boy, that didn't even know me yet. And oh boy, did it just turn out to be that way. Way surreal, that even up to this day, I cannot comprehend the bond Wade and I shared.

At the age of two, Wade started showing tremendous interest in a ball, and started kicking this ball in my Dads kitchen. Even though he was breaking tiles on the wall, he wanted to kick this ball all the time. He even went to bed clutching his ball until he fell asleep.

Growing up, he used to go with my Dad and I to the soccer field in Bosmont, and eventually begged his Granddad to let him put on a soccer kit. Thereafter, he kept nagging his Granddad for tracksuit pants, and asking him to allow him to play.

Eventually my Dad relented and let him play in a game. He didn't do much, except kick anything that moved, including his team mates. He registered that same day at the tender age of two years, to become the youngest football member of the Goretti Football Club, and the youngest ever to register in the Bosmont Football Association. And so began the incredible journey of an unbelievable football talented boy, a talent which was definitely God given.

After playing for six years for Goretti in the Bosmont Football Association, and winning a number of trophies, and Player of the Year award, Calvin Tracy, who was Chairman of Florida Albion Football Club, saw Wadey play, and told me that he had a group of young boys that he would like Wade to play with. Of course we saw the opportunity for Wade and allowed him to go.

Wade scored goals left, right and center, won Tiger of The Tournament at various Tournaments, and people started talking about him in the Rand Central Local Football Association. I watched Wade play, and knew that I had to be involved in his development, and an unbelievable two years passed from the day he left for Albion.

Calvin called me, and asked me to coach the team that Wade was playing in, and to take them to the next level. I saw the team play, and knew immediately that they were a special group of boys. I agreed to coach them, and so the incredible journey and bond between me and Wade resumed and continued until that fateful day.

I was amazed at this awesome group of young boys, wanting to be professional footballers, I had started coaching. They could do anything and everything, that my coaching team and I asked of them. One day, I posed a question to them, of how they would like to be coached . . . 'Like juniors or Like professionals', and without hesitation, they replied "Like professionals, Coach." I knew then and there, that this was a special group of young boys. Needless to say, the rest is history.

And so my story continues . . .

From the time that me and my coaching team started coaching this team of talented young boys, we were beating every team we played, and this wonderful team, in which Wade played, went on to win 25 trophies in just over three years. Gosh, we were getting compliments from the other coaches like, "Where did you get these boys," "Who was coaching these boys," "Where did they learn to play such wonderful football." Believe me; these boys really played wonderful and graceful football. It was a pleasure to watch and coach them. I have coached over 1000 young men and boys in my coaching career, and never have I had a group of boys who gelled so easily together, and exercised, and performed tactics as easily as they did.

Needless to say, on to Brazil we went, to play in 'The Brazil International Tournament' in Rio de Janeiro.

I will never forget the day we left, the excitement in Wade's eyes, the beaming smile on his beautiful face. My word, I still think about it today.

As the plane took off from O R Tambo Airport, Wade sat next to me, on the plane, he grabbed my arm and nervously said, "Uncle Jon, gosh what if we crashed?" I replied, "Then we die, and we die together." That calmed him down, and once we were flying like a bird, I turned and looked at him, and said, "See, it's like riding in a car." All he did was smile, and then, all the boys in our soccer team took over the plane, and really enjoyed the rest of the journey to Brazil.

In Brazil, our boys took the tournament by storm, beating all the teams in our group, and went on to beat their top team in the Quarter-Finals. We were not allowed to drink the water in Brazil, so Calvin had bought bottled water for the boys. Wade did not drink enough bottled water, and ended up in Hospital on a drip, due to dehydration. Gosh, my heart skipped a beat at that hospital, when I looked at Wade lying in that bed in pain. I went down on my knees and prayed to my God to heal him.

After spending half of the day in hospital, he was released. God had answered my prayers. As we got back to our hotel, I got the news that our Captain, Dane was also taken to hospital, also due to dehydration. Later that evening Dane was also released from hospital, but I knew by then that we were going to have problems in the Semi-finals, because I had watched our opponents, their top team played in the quarter final and I knew that they were a pretty good team. The semi-final was scheduled for early the next morning, so there was not enough time for Dane and Wade to recover fully.

Needless to say, before we knew it, we were 2-0 down at halftime. Calvin came over to me, and asked me if there was any chance that Wade and Dane could play. I replied, "Why don't you ask them." He came back to me and said that Wade was willing to play, but Dane was hesitant. I decided to put them both on, and within a short time, we had scored two goals and were level.

But as the match continued, I could see that Dane was tiring, and struggling, but the courage he and Wade showed was amazing. We had numerous chances to score, but just could not, and the opponents went on to score the winning goal, in the dying minutes of the game, and we were knocked out in the Semi-finals.

It was sad to see the boys shed tears openly. I'm not saying that Wade and Dane are the best in our team, but not having the complete team playing from the start, cost us the tournament and I know in my heart that we would have won that semi-final, and gone on to win the Final . . . I suppose it was not meant to be. However, we were awarded the bronze medal on goals scored in the tournament. The boys were rewarded with a beautiful bronze football trophy ball. The joy in their faces at the presentation was unbelievable, and Wade couldn't stop posing with his medal and the trophy. Oh, the joy in my heart, this was one of the proudest moments of my football coaching career.

Back in South Africa and the journey continues . . .

My little star Wade was on the rise. He represented Southern Gauteng in the Inter-District tournament from under 9 to 11 in the SAFA Little League Structures. While playing in the Under 12 Danone Cup tournament, 15 minutes into the match, the Orlando Pirates scout came over to Calvin Tracy and asked him about Wade. Calvin told him that I am the coach and that I'm also Wade's uncle, and that he should speak to me. I in turn told him to speak to Wade's mom who was on the grounds, and they did. She agreed that Wade would join Orlando Pirates Academy.

Wade was so excited about it, but only stayed for two months at Pirates and then told his Mom and myself that he was not happy playing there, for reasons I cannot disclose. He returned to Florida Albion where I continued to coach him.

During the off-season of the RCLFA, Andy, Dane's dad, asked me if he could take Wade to Moroka Swallows in Germiston for a trial. I didn't hesitate and so Wade went. I got a phone call from Andy where he told me to listen in the background, how crazy the Coaches and players of Swallows were carrying on after watching Wade play. Moroka Swallows signed Wade immediately for their academy team. I went on numerous occasions to watch Wade train and play for Swallows junior team. Wade went on to represent Swallows in the Manchester United Nike Cup South African finals.

But one Sunday, going to watch him play, I noticed that Wade was playing against boys much bigger than himself. I asked the Swallows coach what age group it was, and he told me that they were playing under 17. I felt that Wade would not be developing correctly and spoke to the Head of the Academy Mr. Paul Habib about it. He agreed with me and I asked him to release Wade back to me and promised to return him to them once he had grown a bit more.

However Wade's football path took a different direction which meant he could never return to Swallows. At the age of 13 Wade was selected to represent Rand Central Local Football Association (RCLFA) to play in the SAFA Deep South under 15 District tournament.

However, just before this, Wade's life and mine took a dramatic turn by the untimely suicide of Dane, my Captain, and Wade's best friend.

Dane and Wade had become very close in the six months they played together at Moroka Swallows Academy, travelling with myself and Andy, Dane's dad, before Wade left to return to Florida

Albion. Wade was shocked and stunned at what had happened, and was very traumatized by Dane's suicide. He told me that he did not want to play in the tournament that weekend, because he was in no state to concentrate after what had happened. However, we persuaded him to play, and he decided to dedicate that tournament to the Memory of Dane, his best friend. Wade went on to play outstanding football and RCLFA won the tournament.

Wade was named 'Player of the Tournament' where he received the Golden Boot Trophy as reward for his efforts from the Chairman of SAFA Deep South, Mr. Tony Reeves. Wade dedicated that award to the memory of Dane van Schalk, his best friend.

The next day, on Wade's birthday, we laid Dane to rest. I could see the pain and anguish on my little boys face. Gosh, how I felt for him, He cried relentlessly at the funeral and asked me how could

Dane have done this to all of us and especially to Uncle Andy. I replied that only God knows that answer, and that one day he will meet Dane again.

What a traumatic week all of us from Florida Albion had. One of our best boys laid to rest at the tender age of 13. Not knowing in my wildest dreams that my time was coming, to go through the same experience that Andy was going through.

Two months later Wade represented RCLFA again in the Under 15 District tournament at Marks Park and that's where Eric Tinkler asked me if Wade could join the Bidvest Wits Football Centre. Arrangements were made, and Wade, his mom, me, the Chairman of Florida Albion and the Director of Coaching were taken through the process of how things worked at the Centre, by Mr. Eric Tinkler. Wade then signed up to join the Bidvest Football Centre as from the next season.

Wade played for Bidvest Wits for two seasons and it was quite a learning curve for him. The other boys were so much bigger than him, but he was able to hold his own. We received quite a few accolades from Mr. Rodger de Sa, who was the Professional team Head Coach at the time, saying that Wade had an unbelievable talent, and given time, he would go on to be a superb professional player. He also received accolades from various other coaches while playing against them for Bidvest Wits. Wade was part of the Bidvest under 15 Squad which participated for two Years in the Nike Manchester United South African Finals. His proudest moment definitely, was scoring an unbelievable winning goal against Moroka Swallows in the Quarter Final during the 2010 finals at Florida Albion's home grounds.

Wade completed the 2010 season as part of a very successful Bidvest Wits under 15 Team, although he told me that he was not entirely happy with his performances, and that the following year he was going to be on top of his game.

The next year Wade really started with a bang. I watched him play in the first two league games in the Academy league, and could see that he was back to his brilliance, the way I knew he could play. He was outstanding in the second last game of his life where he was voted 'Man of the Match' by the opposition coach. He was so proud and said to me, "See Uncle Jon, I told you I'm going to be on top of my game." I felt proud and just smiled, and said, "Keep on doing that, and the sky is the limit," not knowing that in a short time, my world would come crushing down like a massive earthquake.

AMAZED AT THE GIFT

I was just amazed at my little boy playing with all these boys that were seven and eight years old. Proud was not a word to describe how I felt watching how this child played soccer. Looking at him, I knew that he was special and gifted, not knowing that along this journey, we would find out exactly just how gifted he was and not just in soccer but also in spreading God's love around the world in his short life on earth.

Well, let me get back to that fateful day in 2010. I prayed a lot in my short time after my conversion. But now the 'Rosary' would become a significant part of my life and immediately as we entered that hospital, my 'Rosary' came out, and stayed in my hand with one 'Our Father' and one 'Hail Mary' after another. I never knew that in one day I would say so many Our Father's and Hail Mary's, over and over again. But in this time I never became over anxious, or even felt hopeless, instead I found an unbelievable peace in saying it over and over. Not for one moment did I stop or even think of putting it away. What still surprises me to this day is that even the doctors did not mind me walking in between them saying the 'Rosary' out aloud. I learnt in that time how powerful the 'Rosary' would become and what a significant part a string of beads would play in, not only my life, but in my entire family's lives.

The doctors had started working on Wade at 3pm. By 5pm the Surgeon said that there was nothing they could do for Wade, he was clinically dead, and according to his diagnoses, from an overdose of drugs. Jonathan came to the trauma section to find out how things were going. I told him what the doctor had said. He started crying and so did Demi. I looked at my brother and saw how in such a short space of time, his whole world had crumbled. It was like the earth had opened up and swallowed everything he possessed, and he now stood alone, lost, not knowing which direction to turn. In the meantime Demi had contacted her sister Sheree, and my son-in-law Sufyaan in Mosselbay. They were now crying hysterical. I felt so sorry for my child. I could not comfort her, nor my son-in-law, or my grandchildren, because they were so far away. You can just imagine how helpless she must have felt, her only brother, and she's so far away.

WERE THEY ANGELS IN DISGUISE?

A male nurse came to me and said, "Mummy, don't worry, just continue praying, God will hear your call." That is when I continued praying, and for some reason the other doctors continued working on Wade, and just after 6pm, they took a decision to do a MRI scan on Wade. But, the surgeon was against it. I remember him clearly saying to the one doctor that this child had over-dosed and that they were wasting their time, and that he wanted absolutely nothing to do with authorizing the MRI scan. He said they were wasting their time because even if Wade came around, he would not know who he was or remember anyone, or anything. I immediately binded the comment and my prayers became even more earnest and demanding.

I remember one doctor picking up the phone, and phoning someone to get ready as they were bringing a patient in to check his brain movements. That was when they wheeled Wade into the scanning room for a MRI scan. The radiologist that was on duty, got everything ready, strapped Wade and pushed him in. I in turn walked around her saying my Rosary without fail.

After they had done everything, they pulled him out. She looked at the results, came over to me, and told me that the scan had revealed nothing unusual, and that everything was normal according to the scan. She was quite surprised and looked confused because the scan had not revealed anything.

She turned back to me and asked me to explain what had happened that would cause Wade to be like this. I told her exactly what had happened. She then told me that according to the Surgeon, he was convinced that Wade had over-dosed. I told her that they could do a drug test to check. She looked at me and told me, "Mummy, I see you telling the truth," and with that she went to him to ask him to authorize for blue ink to be inserted, because the previous test showed nothing unusual, but with the ink inserted, it would reveal everything. He declined and refused to authorize the procedure.

Up until today, I am still amazed at what she did after that. She looked at him and told him that she would call the Head of Radiology for permission. He then told her that she could do that, but he assured her that they would decline. I looked at him and thought, "You have absolutely no idea what a Great God we serve," and with that she picked up her cell phone, dialled the number, and walked away. Within five minutes she called in her assistant to administer the drug and within seconds they were busy with Wade again.

MOTHER MARY INTERCEDING

Looking back, I know that God's grace was working in that hospital, and that Mother Mary was interceding like you cannot believe. They worked with so much care and the special attention that Wade received from the doctors and radiologist of the hospital was phenomenal, but I had no idea that what was still to come would be even more amazing than the frontline team.

When they had completed the scan, once again she stood speechless, and could not explain how the test still did not reveal anything. It showed that Wade was normal, nothing abnormal in his test. I remember her looking at me amazed, and saying that she had no way of explaining how Wade could be in this state. All she said to me was that I must not stop praying and God's grace is upon him.

Wade was moved to the ICU ward that very night, and I remember us escorting him. In the meantime all the children had gone to Jonathan's house while we, all the adults stayed at the hospital. My sister Linda, and her partner Cass, arrived as Wade was wheeled into the ICU room. They were busy with more tests and taking more vials of blood, machines were coming in and going out.

My sister-in-law then came in to tell me that she and Jonathan would like to speak with me. So I followed her out of the room. They told me that they had taken a decision, and that they had R100.000.00 and would like to have Wade transferred to Garden City Clinic for the best treatment. I stood back and said, "Jon and Maine, just step back and look around you, what have you been looking at from 3pm, machines that we have never seen before coming to the fore and being used on Wade. Look at the staff, how they have bent over backwards to assist Wade and us. Go to the door and see how many doctors and nurses are working on Wade right now. He is getting the very best at a minimal cost." I stretched out my arms and said, "Look at this, do we really need to move him at an exorbitant price for the same treatment, and here we have such excellent doctors and nurses." Both had to admit that he was getting exceptional treatment, and under no circumstances would I take Wade from here with these phenomenal angels at work. I knew they were doing what God wanted done. I was not prepared to question God on anything. I was just ready to accept what he had in store for me, waiting eagerly to receive.

WERE ANGELS IN PROGRESS?

The nurses were absolutely phenomenal, in normal circumstances they would never allow anyone into the ICU, but in this case, they allowed us all in while they worked on Wade. I was amazed at how they took special attention, and worked on him in such an awesome, caring way. God definitely had a hand in all of this.

As they worked, my sister Linda held Wade's hand, Jonathan stood on the other end with Cass, while I walked around his bed praying the Rosary. Not for one moment did we stop praying while they worked on Wade. You would not believe that Wade had about seven nurses and doctor's around him as they worked relentlessly on him.

As they worked he would start shaking, my sister would then rub his arm and hand, while Jonathan was on the other side holding the other hand. They would speak to him, and as they spoke, I said the Rosary and he would calm down and the shaking would stop. I still have the picture in my head of them working with Wade to do the lumber punch, and because he was so restless, my sister Linda held him down, while I paced the room praying.

I know my sister Linda thought I was afraid, but I knew that my prayers were far more vital and important at that moment, not that I was scared, but because I know that's what my family thinks. I never doubted, I knew in my heart that my prayers and faith was to play a vital role in Wade's recovery. I don't recall much of that test, but the one thing I knew was that it would not have revealed anything, my faith was strong.

While Wade was being hooked up to the machines, I watched how my brother Jonathan walked into the foyer and sank to the ground, crying, holding his head in his hands, questioning how this could happen, saying that he needs Wade, and cannot live without him, and that Wade was his life.

How true those words would be to us in time and what an impact it would leave on our lives later. At that moment, I so hoped that I had an eraser, to erase the last few hours and the pain. These words too, would impact later in our lives, but I knew I had to be the stronger one and not to give in to weakness, or to give up on God, because I knew that if there was any one thing that would pull us through this ordeal, it would be Him, my God. So I turned, and called out to God in my heart for His grace and strength. I turned back to Jonathan, took his hand and we walked back into the private room.

While with Wade, he had a number of seizures in that short space of time. We never stopped speaking to him, and as soon as one came, they stroked his arm, held his hand, and while speaking to him, he would calm down.

Eventually the seizures stopped, and by 11pm he had calmed down completely, and the nurses only needed to monitor him with all the machines hooked up on Wade. They told us we could go home and rest, and if anything changed they would call, because there was nothing else they could do now for him, except to monitor him.

After lengthy discussion, and against all odds, they convinced our family that we needed the rest. We left for home.

PRAYER WARRIORS

Wade's Step-dad, Lawrence, called to say that some people from their church were doing an all-night prayer just for Wade. I knew that with those prayers we had hope!

When I got home I started praying. Prayer never left me, and as I lay in my bed, I asked God to hold my son in the palms of His hands, and to hold him close to His bosom, as I drifted off to sleep.

In the early hours of the morning, God revealed to me in a vision, that as I would walk into Wade's hospital room, he would be up waiting for me, I actually heard him call, "Mom." It was so real, and I remember in my dream that I couldn't believe that Wade had actually called my name. I was so afraid that if he came around, he would not recognize any of us, because I remember thinking back to what that surgeon had said, that even if Wade wakes up, he will not recognize anyone or even remember anything. But I heard God say, "I will give him back to you."

I jumped up. It was only a dream. But such a vivid dream, almost life-like. You can imagine just how real that dream felt, and I knew once again, that God was telling me not to worry, that when I reached the hospital, Wade would be awake.

At that precise moment, my brother Jonathan called, crying, saying he wasn't sure about going to church. He wanted to go to the hospital to be with Wade. I told him to go to church, to light a candle and pray, and that I would go to the hospital.

I woke the children up to get ready for the 10am hospital visit. I couldn't wait to get to the hospital because I knew that Wade would be awake. When we eventually got to Helen Joseph hospital, I went running up the stairs, and what a lot of stairs it was to climb, but I went running up. Demi was ahead of me, she just couldn't wait to get to her brother, with her sister Neliah right on my heels.

We entered Wade's room. He was still in a coma, lying in his cot. My heart sank, because I thought that when I walked in, Wade would be awake and sitting up. But instead of Wade being awake, the man next to Wade, who the night before looked like he was on his last, and could hardly breathe, was sitting up. I thought to myself, last night when I looked at this man, I thought he would not last the night, but instead was breathing on his own, without the assistance of his breathing apparatus, and Wade, was still in a coma.

I was a little bit upset, no actually, my heart was broken. I thought that I'd walk in and find my boy sitting up, given back to me. In my dream I know what God had shown me, but here I was, and nothing had changed.

WAS SHE THE GUARDIAN ANGEL?

As I looked back at Wade, I saw a nurse standing by him, holding his hand and stroking it. She said that he came around for a while and then went back into a coma. She had taken him out of his cot and had sat with him for a while, and just before we came in, she put him back into his cot. She told me that she was a bit upset because they had tied him down because he was very restless, but when she came on duty, she removed the restraints, spoke to him, and that was when he opened his eyes to look at her, and then closed them again. That was when she decided to take him out of the cot and hold him to make him feel safe and comfortable. She had sat with him for quite a while, which was not part of her normal duty. That I felt was definitely an Angel at work and once again, a confirmation about how God works in our lives.

If I think back, I can see clearly how the nurse was dressed, it was not the normal nurses clothing. Could I have imagined it . . . , what I thought I saw . . . , perhaps she was just a nurse? That question will probably live with us for the rest of our lives. I never saw her again after that.

We sat with Wade and once again, I took out the Rosary, and started praying again. I walked around his bed and the old man's bed saying the Rosary relentlessly. It just came flowing out like a river, until the bell rang, warning us that visiting time was over.

DOUBT SETTING IN

As I walked out, it felt like I was betrayed. I started questioning God. There and then, I made a promise to God that I would serve him until death, if He gave Wade back to me, even just for a short while.

Did I know what I was actually asking for; did I even think for a moment what it all meant? No, we never think about what we ask, we just ask without thinking about the implications. But I knew what God had shown me, and I trusted God with my entire being, and I do know that when God shows you something or tells you something, you listen and you wait on Him, and that is what Demi, Neliah and I decided to do, we would trust and wait on God.

I drove to our church and sat outside listening to Pastor Dan preach inside the church. Demi wanted to go in but I told her that I wanted to sit outside and speak to God and Jesus. I was too afraid to question God out loud, even though a part of me wanted to scream out loud saying, "You promised, how could You show me so clearly that Wade was awake," but I knew that if I did, I would put doubt in Demi and Niah's minds. I needed them to trust God implicitly and without a doubt, so I wrestled with God within, and the minute they stepped out of the car at the church, I cried to God telling Him, "You showed me, You revealed it to me, but getting to the hospital, it was the opposite."

The tears welled in my eyes. I cried hitting the steering wheel. It felt good to finally vent some steam. I settled down, started praying again and after a while, started speaking to God and Jesus, told them what was on my heart, and then took out the rosary.

When I completed praying the rosary, I immediately heard a voice saying, "be still and know that I am with you and Wade."

God told me go home, instantly peace came over me. I drove home silently praying inside my heart.

Before we knew it, it was almost visiting time again.

THE FEAR, AND THEN HOLY SPIRIT DELIVERANCE

I can clearly picture it and still thinking about it, sends shivers down my spine. How nervous I was as we prepared to leave for the hospital. Nerves mounting as we drove, and fear creeping in about, would Wade be awake, and would he recognize me or anyone else.

I could not wait to get to the hospital, as we were nearing so the nerves were mounting. I remember feeling my heart beating outside my chest, and within me. I'm trying so hard to calm myself down.

When we arrived at the hospital, we ran to the entrance. All I wanted to do was to get to that hospital room and see that God had kept His promise. As we turned the corner at the entrance, we saw people standing in queues. Anxiousness consumed me, I needed to get in. I wanted to see the miracle He showed me the night before, I needed to calm down. I want to push in and stand right in front, so that I could run up those stairs to my child. Lawrence tells me to stand still and to stop being so restless. Does he have any idea what is going on inside of me, No! Of course not, how could he know the pact God and I have. How could he know what God had revealed to me, and what He had spoken within my heart? No one knew, except me and Demi. Both of us were wrestling with these feelings.

As the security guard opened the doors, Demi, Niah and I went flying past everyone. And I realized how mother and daughters were competing to get to Wade first. Nothing and no one was going to stand in our way as we wrestled all the way up. Sometimes, ok most of the time Demi would be in front of me and when she needed air, Niah and I would overtake her. I was going to make sure that I reached his room first, but I guess at my age, and with my lung capacity, there was no way I would get there first, Demi entered the room first. She screamed, "Mummy! Mummy!" Fear surrounded me. Why is she screaming? As usual, we think the worst. Out of breathe I got to his room, and as I entered, I stopped dead in my tracks. My heart raced and I wanted to scream out loud for the whole world to hear. I stood there, my mind racing, how could this be? Why the doubt? Why the shock? Did I not trust God enough to know He would keep His promise?

I stood in awe looking at my son, he was not just sitting up, looking at me, he recognized me as well, I kept telling myself that my son is sitting up, and as he saw me entering, his first words were, "Mummy, what happened, what am I doing here, how long have I been here?" I ran to him, but Demi got there before me, and grabbed him. Silently, I praised and thanked God from the bottom of my heart. I could feel my heart leaping for joy. I think that if I could do loops, cart wheels, go crazy, and jump from the roof top to tell the world about God's promise to me, I would have, but I knew I had to contain myself.

As I turned to my side, I looked for the old man, he was gone. My heart sank, what could have happened? Just then a nurse walked in and I immediately questioned her regarding the old man. She told us that they could not believe that he had recovered so miraculously, and when the doctors came on their rounds, they were amazed at his recovery and sent him home. At that moment I realised that when you pray prayerfully it can heal not only the person you prayed for, but many others.

My heart did leaps over and over, in awe at God's work. Not only was my Wade awake and knew each one of us, although confused about what he was doing in hospital, the old man was well enough to be sent home and was with his family.

Fast and furiously, family and friends arrived. I recall one particular incident that touched my heart, Andy, Wade's other father, Dane's dad came to visit with his brother-in-law, now look at God's work at hand; this is someone that we never knew but had a relationship with Wade. He loved Wade as if Wade was his own and offered to have Wade transferred to Garden City Clinic and pay for the costs. But I was quite happy with the service we had been receiving from Helen Joseph; they all seemed like angels sent from Heaven.

When the bell rang for us to leave, I was so excited, I had a new lease on life.

THE MIRACLE

God had given my son back to me, and as we drove out of the hospital, I stopped the car, opened the door, and screamed out in a loud voice, "I serve a living God!" I wanted the whole world to know how I felt about God, and what God had done for me, but, did I know, that having such faith would cost me the ultimate price for loving God so much, and that through it, I would be taken to another level of testing beyond any expectation.

No, not for one moment do we ever think about consequences. We often in life take too much for granted, and never think about the implication that comes from a very simple request.

By Easter Monday my son was ready and desperate to come home. Looking at Wade, you would never have thought a day ago my child was clinically dead. According to doctors, he had no chance of survival or a normal life.

The old bubbly Wade was back and ready to go, and that was all due to God, but the doctors wanted to keep him in hospital for another day just to ensure that everything was fine. Tuesday morning we were at the hospital ready to collect Wade, but had to wait because they first needed to do an EEG to ensure that Wade's brain level was normal, and that there were no complications. When all the tests were done we left for home.

Boy! It felt good to be a complete circle again. It scared me a lot knowing that if my son did not make it, our circle of life would be broken.

Could God have prepared or warned me that the circle was about to be broken . . .

Did I not see or adhere to the signs . . .

For the first time in my life I looked at life in a different light. I knew that I would never take anything for granted again, after this major test we had just gone through. I knew that I could only trust God and that I would walk that road and no other road would be good enough for me.

I noticed, and was amazed at the transformation that took place in our home and personal life, and how our faith grew stronger after Wade's near death experience. I was also amazed in the weeks following, how Wade's love for God grew even stronger. I remember him clearly saying to me, "Mom, you really do love and trust God a lot hey, you live for God." I remember how he said that he wants that for himself too.

In the months that followed, Wade would actually come to see how God would work for him.

A TEST IN FAITH

Wade had injured his coccyx and was unable to play the soccer matches preceding the Engen Cup. He was really upset because it would be the last Engen tournament he would be able to play.

"Mom, how can this happen now with my last year for Engen." "Wade, we serve a living God, and that God can make the impossible possible. Trust beyond a shadow of a doubt that nothing is impossible, and you can have the same relationship with God that I have". "But how do you know that God will make it happen?" "Trust in Him Wade, and you will see." He gives me a skeptical look and goes back to playing with his cell phone.

Two days later he comes to me and says, "Mom, you know I believe you, and I trust that God will make it happen." This would come to be true when Wade received the entry form for the Engen Cup,

What I noticed most, was that his love for me took on a different meaning and direction. My son couldn't stop telling me how much he loved me, and that he would never be able to live without me. I also noticed the transformation that took place with my girls. Was what happened to Wade a wake-up call and a reality check? Oh! Yes, I definitely think so. Through that miracle, we saw a transformation in our lives. Our home life started flourishing spiritually, and in every other aspect.

But what I did not know, was that beyond that gift, what would still come to pass, and that the ultimate price we would pay would be life rendering. Still to come would be one of the greatest tests in our love and faith for Christ.

Do we ever think about what we ask for, and do we really and truly thank God for all we have?

I often wonder about that, and at what cost . . .

CHAPTER 2

WADE'S MEMORY BOX

Opening the memory box . . .

I can't do this Lord. You say I have to open the box. I'm afraid of what I might see. I can't write this book. You are making me go back into my inner most, deepest, locked away memories. Memories that I have hidden so far, deep, deep down in the memory box where immense pain and suffering hides, memories that will bring out all the anguish we have had to endure.

I'm holding the key. I'm afraid to unlock the box. Lord, I cannot look into it, I'm afraid of what I will see. Opening Pandora's Box is like opening wounds that have been covered by scabs. But underneath those scabs it is still a very raw and very much an unhealed sore.

Shaking and shivering, I put the key into the key hole and start turning. Fear grips me, can I do this? Lord can I really go down this road. I know I have to do this. Slowly the key turns and the lid pops open. I step back fear gripping me. I'm holding my head in my hands. I'm going into it once again. I'm living the ordeal, something I thought I would never, ever want to endure. Help me Father. Grant me the grace to look into the memory box and let the writing once again come from You.

At 8:55am on the 24th May 2011, the first sms comes through. I'm busy, I cannot read it now. It can only be Wade or Demi, but something is tugging at my heart saying, "read the message." It's a 'please call me' from Demi, instantly panic encamps me. A sudden fear enters me, I can feel it overcoming me. I pick up the phone and I call Demi.

She is scared and afraid, I can hear it in her voice. The words are, "Mummy, Wade is going to commit suicide. He sent a message to a girlfriend and he's left school. He said he was going home to get his tie and will be back. He promised me mummy that he will come back to school. I tried to tell my teacher but she's not interested, and she won't let me go look for him." A sharp pain rips through my heart. Panic sets in. I don't know what to do, don't know who to call. God help me, I'm frantic. Where do I start . . . ?

The first thing I do is call his cellphone. It rings, I'm praying, "Lord let him answer the call. I need to hear him; I need to speak to him, please! please!" Oh boy! Doing this is painful, going down memory lane; it's like a knife piercing through my heart. The pain is excruciating. I can feel that pain ripping through me again. Lord let him answer. Suddenly, I hear his voice, a slight ease in hearing his voice. Thank You Lord, for letting him answer the phone.

"Wade, what's wrong? what are you going to do? you can't do this boy, I need you; we need you. I can't live without you Wade, what will happen to me boy, you are my life. I will not be able to live without you, and what about Uncle Jon?"

This is too much for me. I need to close this box Lord. Pain is ripping through my entire body. I'm holding my head in my hands, my heart is pounding. I can feel it in my chest. I see the beating of my heart on the outside of my chest as I look down. I can't do this, it is just too painful. Please take me from this Lord. Please make this all go away.

"I have to do it mummy," "No, you don't have to do it Wade. You are going to destroy this family if you do it boy, think about me; think about how much I love you. How will I do it without you? you are my right hand, we do everything together; I will not be able to live without you." "I'm sorry Mummy I have to do this. I will come back for you. Tell Uncle Jon I will come for him and Grandpa too."

The call ends. Frantically I dial the number again, but it goes to voice mail. I dial Lawrence's cellphone and I instruct him to go to the house. I explain that Wade left school and he is going to commit suicide.

God help me, I turn to my colleague Norah, "Norah, Wade's going to kill himself, I don't know what to do." She looks at me, fear shows on her face. "I really don't know what to do."

She turns to me and tells me in the calmest of voices "Do what you do best." I tell her I can't; she says, "You can Vee, you always do. Go to the toilet and speak to your God. You know He will tell you where to go."

Getting up, walking to the toilet, once I am inside, I drop to my knees and start praying fervently. "Lord, he can't die now, when I found out I'm carrying a boy, I made a promise to You, a promise I kept, now You need to keep Your promise to me and tell me where to find Wade. Don't let me lose him please God, give me another chance. We have just found our way into Your world as a family. I will never be able to live without him. I prayed for this little boy, we had a deal God, we had a deal!" Fear and panic has consumed me. "Please God, You really need to come through for me now, I need You more now than ever before. Do not forsake me Father." I ask God to hold my son in the palm of His hands, and to direct my path.

Instantly God tells me where to go. Coming out of the toilet I call my brother Jonathan, He says, "Nes, I want to send Romaine to look for Wade but I don't know where to send her." I tell him to send her to the Riverlea Railway line. He says, "ok." He's crying, "No, No! This can't be happening. Not my Wade," and puts the phone down.

I call Lawrence, he's crying, he can't find Wade, he's not at home. I tell him that he needs to go the Riverlea railway line. He asks which side, I tell him just to drive, and God would direct him. Just as I put the phone down, my sister-in-law Romaine calls to find out which side of the rail way line. My instruction is the same as what I told Lawrence, "Drive Maine, you will know where to go."

I'm in the box . . .

I'm picturing everything. I'm living it now. My heart is racing; the knife is going deeper into my heart. The cold is even in my feet. I'm holding my chest. The pain is so severe Lord; I'm crouched to the ground. I have to close the box. I promise I will open it tomorrow. It's just too much for one day, to have to look into it. The unassuming agony that lurks within is unbelievable. Dammit, it's all around me, "Get away from me, leave me alone, you have no right to be here, stop lurking around. I hate you death, I hate that you have invaded my space and taken over my life. A life where God was in control, now suddenly your hand holds my life and you think you have that control. I will not allow you to have that control that only God has the right to." Shutting my eyes from all the agony and reaching over . . . .

Opening the box, I see the pictures of that day floating. I touch the waters, I watch the rippling effect it has and so I start all over again living that day.

Romaine calls Jonathan to tell him she was too late. Wade is gone. He's screaming, going crazy. The phone call comes through; Jonathan tells the receptionist that Wade has just killed himself.

The white dove flies through the office. I can still see the news on the dove's wings and I see in everyone's face, how the transformation of shock and sadness surfaces.

Everyone is in a state of shock. Everybody is going mad. My manager comes running out of the office towards my desk. She walks past all my colleagues telling them that my son just killed himself. She goes to my best friend Tanusha to tell her, shock grips her. She can't move, she needs to get to me, I'm in the kitchen. I see them come running towards me and I know that they all know what has happened. I'm dying inside; I'm contemplating taking my life. Holding me for a brief moment, they say, I'm so sorry. Sorry, what good is sorry, what can sorry do for me? The pain that surges through me, they have no idea, the pain, the loss, the agony within. Sorry! If only I could say, "Take your sorry back and give me my boy." But the words are lost, they no longer important to me. I don't need to hear them now. I only need my son. God help me, take this cup from me, and take me away from here. I can't bear to look at all these people; they have no idea what I'm going through. Open the earth, swallow me in please. I don't want this. It can't be happening, not to me, not to my family. Everybody is in shock. The atmosphere has transformed from happy to sad, and from colours to shades of grey and black. Sadness is everywhere, it's lurking in every corner of the office environment.

Suddenly everyone is picking up phones, calling their kids. One colleague picks up his keys and leaves the office, he needs to see his son at school and tell him that he loves him.

Boy! I'm holding my head again, that is the only relief I have. My heart is beating again, faster than a racing car. My song comes on the radio, I stop. I'm listening to the words, it like's she's looking deep into my heart. She's reading me. I can hear Wade saying through her words, "He's the cloud behind the . . ."

Could he be telling me that he's behind me? I can feel him. I've opened this memory box again. The anguish and pain is surfacing, it's rising. But I know I have to do it. I made a promise to God. I promised I'd open it again tomorrow.

So tomorrow is here and I've unlocked the box. In it I see . . .

THE CLOUD OF DEATH

It has entered every open door, and open window. It has sneakily found its way through every crevice, every opening and slid in under every closed door, closed window, and has rested.

Slowly you see how fear settles in everyone in the office, the fear for their children. Death is here I can feel it; the stillness is all over the company.

I walk to my desk; I open the drawer and take out a hand full of pills. Norah sees me taking it, "No! Vee, you can't do this, It's not right. You are God's child that is what you always tell me." "No Norah, you don't understand, that child was my life, I have to do it." "No, you don't." "Yes, I do Norah." She comes over, tries to take it from me. "Don't, please, I need to die. I won't make it Norah, not without Wade." "You will Vee; you always say God never gives you more than you can handle" . . . "but I can't handle this Norah, I can't."

I want to scream. I want to go crazy, but I can't express my pain. I have to contain myself. "Lord, help me, tell me what to do. My world's crumbling Lord, I have no control."

Suddenly I hear God say "As long as I have control, you will be ok."

31

I try to compose myself. I promise Norah that I won't take the pills. I'm lying, I'm still contemplating it. I hide the pills in my sleeve, as soon they all move from my desk I'll sneak to the bathroom and take it. I need to be alone, why won't they all just leave me alone? so that I can do, what I need to do. I need to get away from this office, from the staring, the questions in their mind. I know what they are thinking. I need to get away from this world. "You know God; You probably know my intentions and You stopping it. Why would You stop what I'm thinking of doing? You know my pain, You knew it before it was about to happen. So leave me, just leave me to do what I intend doing. Even if not now, that's ok, I'll get my chance."

I pick up the phone and call my sister Linda, and I tell her. I can hear her screaming. It is silent. I dial my cousin Brenda and give her the news, she's in shock, and I hear her screams . . . "No! no!, this can't be happening."

Then, the silence once again . . .

The cloud of death moves over to Wade's school, not only over JSS High School, but Wade's Primary School, T.C. Esterhuysen as well. Mr. Vergie the principal, and the staff of T.C. Esterhuysen are in total shock. Demi is with Mr. Arthur in the principal's office of JSS High School when I call, to give her the news, they are in shock. Everyone is crying. Wade's friends are going crazy. They are taken to the office for assistance. They cannot comprehend this, the friend, the footballer, the joker of the class . . .

Nadira, Wade's house friend is lost, "What am I going to do? my confidante, the brother I never had." Death has left them speechless and in tremendous pain. They will definitely require counseling after this news. The school is in disarray.

The cloud of death has now left the schools and has moved over to the Bidvest Academy. At the Academy, the boys are training when they receive the news of Wade's death. All training has stopped;

death has rest there for a while and will move to where I'm going. All the boys are taken in and tears are shed.

How I hated that day, because with that day came a lot of pain and suffering that will probably last a life time. But what I hated most, was the cloud of death, it just leaves behind pain where it rests. It has torn our family apart. "Lord, Your help is needed here, where do we go from here. How could this have happened Lord?"

"Our memory box is filling up Lord. The water level is rising. Father, You will shortly have open the box to release some tears into the river. The box is so full and heavy; Oh Lord, the heaviness is dragging me down." Did Wade ever think of the heaviness, sadness and loneliness he would leave behind?

My office phone rings, but I have already left for home. Tanusha, who was on her way to my desk answers the call. It is Lawrence calling, and he wants to speak to me. She tells him that I've just left. He cannot contain himself and breaks down weeping uncontrollably. He is so emotional and helpless.

For her to actually hear a big man cry so much is disconcerting, all she hears him say is, "I'm too late" and, "Where is Venessa? I want her," and cries. It also breaks her heart knowing that she would no longer see this child, so handsome, growing up in front of her eyes, and there was not a thing she could do to contain or comfort the family. It's the worst feeling anyone could imagine, was the words of my friend.

As I walk, pills fall from my sleeve, one by one, leaving a trail. But the chance never comes for me to do what I'm thinking of doing. As one falls another follows, and that's how it goes until I'm in the company vehicle, and I'm being taken to the place of death.

The journey to the 'place of death' is taking forever. My mind is blank. I can't think, only emptiness inside. "What do I do when

I get to 'that place' what awaits me Lord? I have no idea. Help me to walk this bravely. Father, grant me the strength so that I may be strong for all."

When I arrive at 'that place' the cloud of death has already rested with the cold and will stay for a while. I don't feel the cold seeing all the people, I only feel death, and I know that it will be here for a while. I take a deep breathe; I'm contemplating closing the box. I so desperately want to hold my head but I know I have to do this.

I jump out of the vehicle and run to the lane where my son lays. They intercept but I'm screaming, "I want my child, I need to hold him." They hold me and try to take me away. I grab hold of the police vehicle bumper. "Nes, you don't want to see him like that, he's bad, remember him the way he was." "I don't care; I want to see him, he's my child. I will kill anyone who tries to take me away." I hold on for dear life. The police will not release me to go to my son.

Oh! Lord the pain in my chest is there again. I'm holding my head, the only reliever I know. After what seems like forever, I let go and I walk into the crowd. I see Jonathan collapse. People everywhere, "Why don't they just go Lord, this is my privacy, me and my family nobody else." I see how Deidre, Wade's friend, Joshua's Mom, who we called Wade's weekend Mom, takes Jonathan and holds him. I see my sister Linda, my cousin Brenda, and so many others in the distance. I want to die. It would be easier to die than to be here. I will feel no pain, I will not have to answer to anyone Lord, not a single person.

As I walk back to the car, I see the trail of the yellow pills, and I drive home in silence. Death, silence and cold follows me. To this day that silence is with me, and it goes where I go. But the most amazing thing is that till this day, I have never needed to account to anyone. That is how my God works; He looked into my heart and read my words.

And once again I'm touching the waters to get a clearer view of what the memory box holds. At the same time my thoughts go to whether we will ever accept the inevitable of what life has handed us. Suddenly fear wraps its ugly arms around me, turning my head away for fear of what is in store for me, "You have to look Venessa, you have to continue."

So, I do as I'm told turning back, I see it most clear, how Wade . . .

PASS THE BALL

You definitely passed the ball alright, I see it coming towards me at an alarming rate, and with a great force, and I know I have to catch it. The one last chance to have Wade, can't let it slip through my fingers. But the force and speed that it's coming with, I'm afraid I'm not going to take that ball. Jumping, and thinking I just have to grab the ball, but with that speed, it spins through my fingers leaving the finger tips burning. Ouch! fingers burning, rolling them into the palms of my hands, and placing them to my chest, I drop to the ground, turning around I see the ball flying into the distance. I know I've lost you Wade, there is no way Lord I would have caught that ball, with that force and speed.

The game I thought we played was not played fair. It was just highly impossible, and You knew I would never be able to take that ball. I've lost the game, and in the process lost Wade. You gone Wadey, gone, and there is absolutely nothing I can do. Wishing I were bigger and stronger so that I could have caught the passing ball, I would have had you in my hands. Holding my hands, the tears starts welling; I know I've lost the toughest game I've ever had to play. Tears rolling, opening my hands, the tears drop onto my burning finger tips, and rolls into the palms of my hands, I see the reflection of Wade's face in the tears. No! God No! Please! Please! Give me one more chance, I don't know how to live without Wade.

You cannot take him from me, please just one last chance at that shot.

Wiping the tears from my eyes, I promise, when he passes the ball, I will definitely catch it, hold it and never let it go. God, You have to help me, I'm lost, and the longing for my son gets worse with each day. Lifting the burning fingers to my face, tears consume me, and knowing that it's impossible, and the inevitable has taken place . . .

I look back to see if I can still see the ball, but instead . . .

THE SNAP SHOT

. . . Comes to life, damn, this is making me relive this nightmare. "You are not going to give me a second chance, are you? What You saying is, I've ran out of penalties, and I have to accept, and that I have to go back to complete the game, through the tears, and boy! are they rolling, with no way of stopping this, because as You say, I have to go through it and complete it." Wiping the tears from my eyes, we arrive at home. Many follow, family, friends, and most of the Florida Albion parents and players. They would all come to play a significant part, as well as Bidvest, in the funeral of Wade.

I hate this Lord; the tears are welling up again, the need to find myself. Why this, why my family? the circle is broken, a piece of my heart is gone forever. Pain pours from the broken piece of my heart. I see it running I cannot stop it. I take the snap shot, and I'm looking at it. It is so sad to see the bleeding from the heart.

People are streaming in and out. I don't know them, but they all seem to know my Wade. It's amazing; in his short life he touched many people, young and old. How could this be possible? Where did you find the time Wade? you only lived fifteen years, but you have touched thousands of people.

I need to hide, I need to find my place and speak with God. I need to find Jesus, where are You? In all this, I stand dead still; I look past all the people. If only through all these people I can find Wade, Jesus, if only. I pray that they would leave so that I can feel my loss, I need to feel it. God, I need to understand it.

I'm in another world, not here. I don't know what's happening. God give me the strength to handle this. I walk into Wade's room and I lay down. There is nothing inside of me, no feelings, and no emotions. I can't do this; I can't be out of control. I need to control this situation, so I get up and walk out. God, let Your hand guide me through all this.

Jon is not doing well, so they call in a doctor. Dr Marlon arrives but he cannot give Jonathan anything, he is too emotional, and too traumatized by the death. Dr Marlon decides against medication.

Everybody leaves, only me, my thoughts, the cold, and the silence are left behind. I know death is everywhere, you can feel it as the silence falls. I kneel and through all this, I call out to God. "Lord, strengthen me as I know that this walk is between You and me." I never quite understood why I said it. Once again I'm asking and saying without thinking it through. But one thing I know is that it definitely did become a journey I would walk alone with God.

Did God prepare me the year before with . . . ?

THE IMPRINT

It's imprinted in my memory. I touch the waters, and again the rippling effect comes to life, anxiousness, the beating of the heart starts, and I know that I've unlocked the memory box.

It is early Wednesday morning, the 25th May 2011, I wake up crying. It feels like my heart is failing, and I lay quietly weeping.

My pillow is soaked with tears, holding my chest, the pain I feel is excruciating, I'm going to have a heart attack, the pain is just too much for me to handle. I want to die; it will be easier for me. God, I can't do this, take me away from here, relieve me from this pain. I need to go to church; I need to speak with God, Jesus and the Holy Spirit.

It is 4:30am. We get into the car and drive to our church, St Maria Goretti Catholic Church in Riverlea. The gates are locked, I'm screaming, I need to go into the church, I really need to go in. I desperately need to speak to God. I call Father Tomas to open the door, only the deadly silence of the early morning replies to my calls. I'm grasping, holding onto the gates, I need to find that peace that you can only find in a church.

Silence rips through the early morning call, with no reply. "I need You God, I need to feel You." I ask Him to take the pain away until after the funeral. I break down and go on my knees weeping. Lawrence picks me up and put me back in the car. As he drives, I feel God's presence envelope me, and peace comes over me.

We drive home and a deadly silence follows us. This deadly silence follows me all around. Does anyone know what a ticking time bomb is inside of me? Does anybody know the war that is waging? and does anyone have an idea of where I am right now? No! nobody at all, only You God, only You know.

As I enter the house, God's strength fills me and I have the energy to tidy the house, before anyone comes. Wade's death is inside of me, I feel that deadly death, as it eats away at me. My sister Linda walks in, the death walks in with her. She goes straight to Wade's room, anger bursts from her, exploding into millions of pieces as she hits the walls and doors screaming, "Why! Wade, why?"

I watch in silence, the deadly pain that rips through us. The unanswered questions start forming, and as people roll in, so the unanswered questions come too. As Jonathan walks in, an even deadlier death walks in with him through the door. The tears roll uncontrollably, and once again, I can see how the waging war of a suicidal death engulfs us. "Oh! Lord, this is unbearable, how do we make it through this day. God, You have to take our hearts and hold it in the palm of Your hands. Please take our hearts and hold it for us."

To my amazement, Linda calms down, and so does Jonathan. And so our duty starts to plan Wade's funeral. I'm dreading the nights, the looks on the faces that will come from the unasked questions, that looks at us, but will never be asked. They will hang there in mid-air, unasked and unanswered not only to us, but to all, baffled by this suicide.

I cannot do anything today, I'm just too tired Lord. This cross that I carry is just too heavy for me. What makes You think that I can carry this cross Lord? You carried it Lord, and we all saw the struggle it was for You. You fell along the way and endured so much, but what about me Lord? I'm tiny in body and in spirit, how do I carry this?

That imprint of need for the Lord will stay within this broken heart.

As we turn, a picture of . . .

THE RADIO STATION

. . . Appears, I'm wondering why? How strange, a picture of a radio station would surface, why would this happen? My cell phone rings, it is Thursday morning, 26th May 2011. I look at the number, it's my sister Linda calling. I look at the time and it is just after 7am. "Nessa, Timmy called to say they are having a talk on Wade's suicide on Rainbow radio station and that we should listen." We jump up and run to the car because that is the only place that we can catch that frequency. As the radio goes on, I hear Wade's dad talking, telling them that there was no sign in his home. I start dialing Rainbow's number but it's engaged, I try a number times, but it just stay's engaged. I'm thinking that perhaps I have the wrong number. I call Wade's dad, he gives me the number and tells me not to be rude because of what all the callers are calling in to say, that suicide starts in the home.

They are afraid I'll be rude. They assume that I'm angry because of what is being said. My mind is racing, I'm wondering, "Did it come from within the home?" Suddenly I remember the question Wade's friend Imtiaaz asked, "Aunty Nessa, how could Wade do this, he was so gifted, he had a home with so much love, all every child would want is what Wade had." That is one thing I keep locked away in the back of my mind and heart. I promise them that I won't be rude.

Lawrence dials the number, but before dialing, they make me promise, that I won't be rude if I get through. They have no idea that I'm praying, and asking Jesus to intercede for me. And once again, I do what I'm so good at doing, I ask God without thinking, that if it is His will, let me get through, and that He should speak through me. I tell them they should just listen to what I have to say, they have nothing to worry about.

A sudden calmness comes over me. I am no longer afraid from looking into the memory box. I can start feeling the tension leave me. It's feeling a lot easier to write now, why is it Lord? that when I'm in Your presence, and I'm busy in the box, the fear and pain subsides, and I'm not afraid to look into the box and touch the waters. But when I'm no longer in Your presence, and I go into the box, the fear is back and I'm afraid, like now I can still feel the pangs luring behind because I've allowed doubt to enter, they are for some reason pushing through the calmness. The beating is starting. I can feel it through to my chest. It's beating into my throat. I'm rather going to close this now, I need to rejuvenate, and I need to recompose, I just need to close the memory box for a while. "You have not finished this chapter, go back and open the box." "Lord, I cannot open it anymore, its just too painful." Slowly I reach for the handle throwing the lid open. Lawrence and Demi's eyes are glued to me. Boy, this is so very hard. "Ok Lord, I need Your help here, remind me . . ."

Touching the waters, my fingers run through it slowly, the picture starts surfacing, oh my word . . .

THE MESSAGES

The messages are coming through. Lawrence and Demi's eyes are still glued to me; I know exactly what they thinking as I start speaking. All I remember, is saying, "My name is Venessa, I'm Wade's mom." Suddenly I'm gone; I am no longer here until I switch the cellphone off. I turn to look at Lawrence and Demi, they are in shock, no-one says a word. I look at them and I ask them, "What's wrong? How did I . . ." no words come out.

The cellphone rings, its Wade's dad. He's crying uncontrollably, telling me that it was so amazing and thanking me. "Lawrence, Demi, what did I do, tell me." The cellphone rings again, it's Clint, he's weeping, "Venessa, you were amazing, thank you." By now I'm confused, what actually happened, tell me what just happened? Timmy calls, and says, it was so touching. Just then the phone rings, it is Althea, "Venessa, everyone at our office stopped working and listened, they're crying. One of my colleagues asked me to call you to say thank you, all these years he blamed himself and turned away from God, but now he can go back to God."

I'm stunned Lord, what just happened here, I need to know. The calls are rolling in, people are weeping. What did I say to get this response, I'm in shock.

Later that evening, I'm getting ready for church, I notice Dr Marlon, and I'm thinking that he's probably here for Jonathan. I turn to ask him if he has seen Jonathan, he says to me, "I've seen Jonathan, but I'm here to speak to you." I stop dead in my tracks, "Me, have I done something wrong Doctor?" "No, actually I came to say, thank you." "Thank me for what Doctor?" "Thank you for taking Rainbow to another level. We have been inundated with calls, my e-mails are full, and I cannot receive any more messages as my message box of my personal mail as well as rainbow's is inundated with requests for the recording. We have had requests for copies of the show from all over, even as far as Cape Town. You went over the time limit but Pastor Humphrey's said to leave you to speak, by the time you were finished, we were all in tears and had to close the show, all were too emotional to continue, we had to take time out to re-coop and find ourselves. The research we've been doing, you have given us new insight into suicides." I'm in shock. What did I say?

Days after the call to the show, people were thanking me for the message, and telling me how it has helped them understand and look at children in a different light. But nobody would say exactly what I had said. I needed to contact Rainbow to get a copy. Timmy called to say that she had ordered a copy, well, at least now I'll get to hear what I had said.

I understand now why I had said that this walk is between God and myself, I never quite understood why I said it before. I see it now in everything that's going on around me.

Children are coming in and out, crying and speaking about the tragedy and their feelings. Many parents are concerned about their children's feelings. It's amazing to see how God starts to work through me. Antonio, Wade's friend's mom, says we should be comforting you, instead you are comforting us.

Even though in the beginning I often thought about those words, slowly I started to comprehend why those words were spoken. They would become a part of me on this road Wade had set out for us.

A few weeks later my sister Linda, called Timmy to find out about the recording, she told us Humphrey would not give copies to anyone, it was too 'sensitive' and that he would only give a copy to Wade's mom. So I went to Rainbow, but I was declined a copy even though I was Wade's mom because of the 'sensitivity' of it.

I would have to rely on Charlene as to what had transpired. Here is what she had to say . . .

THE TRANSCRIPT

I'm getting goose bumps just thinking about that day; it's opening all those wounds. I've been so close to the situation and because it was so fresh after his death, all the talks that morning on Rainbow had me in tears. I really couldn't drive properly. When you came on, I was close to the Pick n Pay on Goldman road, I got such a shock and I immediately turned the car around and went to park right in front of Rainbow. It was like I wanted to be as close as possible to that place and I even felt like going in and saying, that's my Aunt talking, and Wade was my . . . my baby. When you spoke I literally sobbed in the car. All I could say was "Oh! Nes, Oh! Wadey, Why! Why?" over and over. I don't think I could really focus on the strength you gave and shared, all I could feel was the hurt, anger and pain for what had happened.

I saw a number of people crying while driving that Thursday, all of that just flashed before me. I could not think straight. When you finished your talk, I remained parked there for about 30 min, I could not drive. When I eventually drove off, I remember pulling over at St Catherine's school because I was crying all that way, and could not see, so I pulled over to try and recollect myself.

You also spoke a lot about the fact that there aren't always signs. Most people would say afterwards, but they noticed this and that, you said, it isn't always like that. You described how Wade was as normal on his last day, and that he ate normal and nothing out of the ordinary, except that he was over affectionate towards you. You spoke about your relationship with Wade, Wade's relationship with Jonny, Grandpa and people in general, so how could a boy like this do that, it seems so impossible. You spoke about our reliance on God and that if you didn't have God, you would've taken your own life too. You said it's only through God that you can get up each day and get through the day. They asked you, "How do you do it," You answered, "Only because of God."

Oh! Thank you, I'm so glad, I closed the darn box. I can't look into the box anymore, the water has just too much to reveal. Closing it for now is the best thing, because I'm holding my head. This, which I'm doing, is just too much for me. Tears are welling and slowly they start trickling. "It's not fair God, why have You given me this cross, it is all too consuming, and don't You understand that I will never be able to live with it, leave it, shake it, or let it go. Why me Father, why did this happen to me? Will I ever be able to let it go and move on?" Tears are gushing out, it's like they can't come fast enough out, and as they push through fast and furiously, I call out God, "Help me!" The pain is unbearable. I thought looking into the memory box was getting easier but that would be a lie. Was I hoping or imagining it? because suddenly I am reminded that it's actually getting more difficult than ever before.

Memories are flooding in, trying to hold it back, afraid the box will not hold the tears and then the inevitable happens, I let it run. Father, all I have of Wade is memories. I need to hold them close to my heart. The pain becomes intense and goes right through my chest into my heart. The pain is, Oh! so unbearable, "Forgive me Father if I close the box for now because of the pain. Help me Lord! Help me to do what You are asking, it is peeling my heart open layer for layer, and with every layer I peel off, I peel a part of me too, with so much pain, anger, hatred and loss. You say I need to do this Lord, why? What will I gain from peeling layer by layer of my memories that I hold so close to my heart? It's mine Father, my pain, my heartache, my loss." "No Venessa, it's not yours, it's ours. I am here to take it from you." "No! You can't take it Father." "It's for me to carry Venessa, because I am Your Father."

I'm agitated, You are allowing me to wage in this waters. Chaos is everywhere. I have to close this box. I'm sorry Lord, I have to keep my eyes closed, the thoughts are killing me, desperation fills me, desperation for my son, I'm thinking, You saved Lazarus, could my faith be strong enough for that kind of miracle? You did it once, why not again? I'm telling myself, that only happened in the Old Testament, but my faith is like the Old Testament.

Realization knocks at the door, I have to open it, have to be realistic, he's not coming back, and I have to find a way to live with it. If only I had an eraser, I would erase the last three years. While writing this book I'm in a mess. Tomorrow maybe I'll be stronger to continue.

Your grace thus far, is sufficient . . .

GOD, WERE YOU WITH WADE?

It's Thursday 27th May 2011, the memory box is closed, but the water is pushing through. It's all around the box, I'm looking into the water. There it comes again, pictures floating. I have to brave this out, I look into it . . .

I'm on my way to arrange his funeral. We get to Kerr's funeral Parlor, I want to see my child, but they are advising me against it. Jonathan and Linda say no, they convince me not to. I remember Wade's dad and Andy, Dane's dad, saying its better not to go, and that I will not like what I see, I should remember him the way he was.

We leave, but within my heart I know I have to do this. By the afternoon, I know that it is the right thing to do. I tell Lawrence that I want to go, everybody tries to convince me not to, but I walk to the car, I turn around, and in a loud clear voice I say, "No f**king one will stop me, come hell or high water, I will see my child." For a mother, no matter what, it's your child, good or bad, ugly or nice, they are precious. "Venessa, I don't understand why they don't want you to see Wade, he's your child." "Exactly, he's my boy, I need to do this Lawrence, and I need to find closure." Boy! Do you ever find closure . . . ?

I am preparing myself mentally for the worst. How could it come to this? I need to see Wadey. Tears are welling up in my eyes. "Venessa, are you prepared for this?" I ask myself. But I know that no matter what, I have to see my child one last time. The fear is luring there of what I might see, but I know I have to do this, and as we drive, I lift the lid of the memory box. I'm angry at them, and at the world. What a lot of sadness in the box, tears are rolling; I run my fingers through the tears in the box, back and forth, until we arrive. "Lord, are You here?, don't leave; give me the strength to accept whatever my child looks like."

It's 4:30pm when we arrive at Kerr's funeral parlor. They try to talk me out of viewing Wade's body. Nobody is going to stop me; I am staying here until I've seen my child. And after a lengthy debate on whether or not I can handle what Wade looks like, against all odds, they eventually give in.

Stepping through . . .

THE OPEN DOOR TO . . .

The door opens, bravely, without fear I walk in. They bring my son to me. "Oh! No! What am I going to see? Oh! my God am I ready for this," I know what you would look like after a train has bumped you. I have no idea what I am in for, all of the sudden I'm no longer afraid, fear has eluded me, and a sense of peace is here as they pull off the cover. I know I'm going to see the worst ever, but I'm ready, and what I see, is amazing. God, You were there, just like my prayers. You kept Your promise, if only You could have spared his life . . .

Wadey, is complete, how can this be, am I imaging this. They told me he was very bad, but every thread of hair is there, his ears, nose, eyes, his body is almost complete. Quietly I close my eyes and bow my head, tears trickling down, silently I say, "You promised You'd be there, You definitely had Your hand over my son Lord, thank You." I'm in shock could this be real, I blink my eyelids to make sure I'm not seeing things. Walking out of the room saying thank You Lord, turning around walking back into the room, the need to look again as for a confirmation, my son is there. Could this be what God wanted me to see?

I'm staring, and I hear Lawrence say, "I told you Venessa, I don't know what they saw, because even when he laid on the track, I saw Wade, every part of our boy." Instantly I knew that God had kept His promise to me once again. Forgive me God for doubting, I flip the lid close. I'm feeling ok, my heart has settled, no pain at all from looking into the memory box. Thank You God for going ahead and preparing this for me.

Baffled by the suicide, I'm in tears, I wonder if this memory box will burst. I can't hold back, I let it go . . . I run my fingers through the memories that are overflowing. I'm trying to think back, did it come from within the home? I can't seem to find anything or even a change in Wade that indicates it could have come from inside. No confirmation, all I remember is Monday night the 23rd May when he spoke to me, telling me his inner most feelings, and saying that he needs to write a letter for school.

Little did I know that he was writing a letter to me, remembering his words, "Mom, I wrote you a letter, it's in the house." The letter, that's a mystery never to be revealed. Eyes pressed closed together, I'm holding my head again. It seems to be the only comfort I find or get at this time. I've learnt to block out everything, and see nothing. Nothingness is far easier to handle than all the thoughts. I prefer keeping them closed. When they open I see the memory box, and everything comes flooding through, but when they closed, I am painless. I'm getting used to living without feelings, its better that way, no emotions, no hurt.

The day is here for laying my boy to rest, but will we have that rest. It is over flowing, even though the box is closed, the water is gushing out. I'm trying to contain this, hoping the box can hold the tears, so that I can close it and hide it. No way, it's pushing through. "You will never be able to hide it, just open it Venessa, and let it flow." I know exactly what I'm going to see, chaos, and from that, the devastation that will remain with us as we lay Wade to rest. Looking at this Lord is just too much. I'm trying to close the box but can't seem to reach it. Lord, it's out of reach.

Gosh, this church is so full, can't it just be me, You Lord, the family and Wade. Oh Lord, how different this could have been. No one will understand this pain, the loss of a child. No parent should bury a child. People are streaming in from all over; the streets are full, as we leave for the church. Gosh! cars are everywhere. As we are nearing the church there are cars and people everywhere.

We enter the church gates, people fill the inside and outside. There is no space. I know death and silence follows behind. "Leave me! you have no place here, stop following me." I hate the silence, it's a killer, why can't the earth just open and swallow me in, because that would be easier than having all this sadness and questions surrounding me.

Questions are flying through the air. Lord I'm not taking one, it has no place here. Everybody is crying. Nobody understands this senseless death. How could this end like this? Soccer delegates starts streaming through. Tears are rolling, my box can't hold the tears, and I see how it runs over and joins us on the waters. Emotions are high, and I'm afraid of the quiet after this. The quiet is dangerous, it brings thoughts.

Thoughts that so often change the course of our lives and with that . . .

CHAPTER 3

THE AGONY

. . . Of the cold that no longer follows me, but has somehow managed to crawl right inside of me. I can't breathe, my lungs hurt as I grasp for air. My head is ready to burst, and fever has also found its way into this torn, worn out and broken body. Is death here? Oh! How I would welcome it. The pain is also a killer not just mentally, but physically. Was all this just too much for my body, has it taken its toll, has it decided to give up? Lord, the heart is even worse than the body. They rush me to hospital. I have a touch of pneumonia.

The body and the soul are exhausted. "Wade, your death has just been too much for me, for us. Do you have any idea of the suffering we are enduring?" Lying in bed gives me so much time to think. "God, do You have any idea how helpless I felt on that fateful day as he walked out of my life and into Yours? I felt trapped and powerless. No! not felt, I was all that and more, that I could do absolutely nothing for my son. My hands were tied God. I could not wrap my arm around him to make him feel safe and loved and to tell him that everything will be ok, and that a Mother's love is sufficient."

Fear grips me once again, I allow my emotion to take control, and as I close my eyes, the tears roll down the side of my face onto the pillow. Fear enters me, I don't want to close my eyes, and I'm scared Lord. I don't want to fall asleep. "I miss you so much Wadey. I don't want to let you go." I get up, I kneel down, head bowed, and rocking back and forth, my prayers are fervent, and the tears flow freely.

Walking into Dr Kola's rooms he looks at me and says, "How are you doing Venessa?" instantly tears starts forming, Oh! Lord, I'm going to break down, the box is open, and there's nothing I can do about it. I have no control over it, "And the family and your sister Linda?" "Dr Kola, you have no idea of the mess we are in, no one can handle this." He looks at me, "It's ok Venessa; we've known you all our life. I knew Wade since he was a baby, it's ok to cry." "Dr Kola, how could Wadey do this to me, I need to understand this, he was my child, my life, the reflection of who I am. How am I going to make it?" You need counseling Venessa." "Doctor Kola, no counselor will know what's inside of me, they'll never understand, only God understands and knows this pain." Tears are streaming and I have no control over it, I'm just wiping it away. "It's ok Venessa." "Oh! No! Doc, it isn't, it will never be ok. Doesn't anyone understand that nothing will ever be ok after losing a child?"

Dr Kola has no idea that he just opened that damn box. He allows me to express all that is inside of me. Dr Kola suggests anti-depressants, "It will help you to cope." "No, Doctor, I need to go through this, to deal with this at hand. I want to feel every bit of the trauma. I really need to feel it. The need to hold onto the only thought that keeps Wade alive within me. You cannot take the last little bit of whatever I feel for my child away from me now. It will drive me insane not able to feel the anguish, it's the only thing keeping me sane at the present moment. Do you think suppressing it will make it better? No, it won't, it will only make it harder and more difficult to comprehend and handle at a later stage. I need to deal with this anguish now. I don't want to only go through it a few years down the line." There I go again talking without thinking.

Whether now or a few years later I realize . . .

THE REALITY

. . . Is that it's over; I have to face the reality of life. Can I, and will I make it Lord? suddenly I'm afraid to face the world, I'm scared. The fear rises, it's like I looked into the memory box. I'm not touching that water; I want to get away from it. I'm sinking, I can feel it. I'm coming up for air; I'm in the real world. I want to go back under, it's better there, it's somehow feels safe. But I know I have to come up.

As I surface, I'm facing everyone. Boy! I'm being brave as I walk in, I'm hoping for sympathy, but instead, I get a wakeup call. Reality hits, and I know later it will come back to remind me, that even though what seemed like heartless, with no empathy, it will become my crutch, and help me to handle the situation. But right now, at this moment, I know that at this stage of my life, I can't handle the reality of life. I need to be home, in my safe haven.

While driving from work in the taxi, looking out of the window, I no longer see the beauty of this world, all I see is shades of grey. I have lots of anger and hatred inside of me. I've been robbed of my only boy; I need to find a way to work through it. I close my eyes and say a silent pray, "Lord, help me, help me to once again see the beauty, to love life, and to change the shades of grey to colours, please help me find it."

"You have to surface Venessa, and face it head on, you cannot hide from your fears and people." "But I'm not ready." "Whether you like it or not, you in this, and facing it head on will help you." "Doesn't anyone understand, even if life continues, what about me, where do I fit into all this?" Suddenly I'm pushing the glass door open, I've stepped onto territory that I once felt familiar in, suddenly now, I'm not sure. Don't look at me, and don't even think of saying a word.

The tears have been there all morning, if anyone says something to me now, the lid will pop. Walking to my desk is such a mission because I can feel the looks, and I know their thoughts, they are dying to say, "Vee, how are you coping?" "I'm not coping Father, I'm not ready to face the world. I still need to feel this loss, to absorb all this. I need my safe haven, that's the only place where peace and comfort is." Sitting at my desk, could anything be this hard to do? The lid pops open, I see how the heart is ripped open, and the pain that comes from it is staggering, it's like someone has pierced the heart with a knife and ripped it right through. Silently the tears drop on my desk, it forms a puddle. Somehow Norah (Nthabiseng) my colleague, knows I'm crying, she slides her chair back, looks at me, instantly her eyes fills with tears, she gets up from her chair, walks around to my desk and embraces me, I feel her strength enveloping me and whispers in my ear, "You so strong Vee, your God has made you a phenomenally strong woman, if it was me I would not be here today." Wiping the tears from my eyes and then hers, she steps back and says in a strong yet gentle voice, "Do what you do best Vee." "How can I do this Norah? when I'm in such a mess, trying so desperately to hold onto God, but it feels like I'm failing." "You not failing Vee, you just have a lot to handle. I know you, and I know how you feel about God, so just do what you do best." Looking at her with tears in my eyes, I have to get to the bathroom.

The bathroom is just around the corner; walking to the bathroom I see how the puddle of tears leads the way. "Please Lord, let the bathroom be empty." Pushing the door open, silence greets. It surrounds me, and once again, I know you are with me. For some reason you just like following me. I hate it so much, because from that comes the lonely, and the reminder that the silence will always be a part of me. Running into the cubicle, closing the door, dropping to my knees, the tears have escaped; it has found its way through. The puddle finds its way under the door, stops in front of me, and slowly the little droplet from my chin drops into the puddle. I know where you going, you going to join the others in the box, and sooner or later, you'll flow into the river and join Wade on the waters. "God help me, I'm going crazy, all this is just too much. I'm not supposed to be here, how did this happen, that I could lose a son, if I loved You more God?" Looking up to the heavens, tears streaming down, "Explain this to me, because I'm losing my mind." And dropping my head to the ground, I weep with all that is in me.

Getting up, wiping the tears, walking out of the bathroom, stepping into the reality of what life has handed me, I walk to my desk. My boss comes, he looks at me, and walks away. I know what he is thinking, I know he understands and gives me a moment to find myself, and through that, God gives me the strength. "You can do this Vee, God has always been with you." "I know Norah, it's just that I need to fathom this, to comprehend this senseless death." And as the tears form in the eye lids and drop, I do what I'm supposed to do, and that is work.

When those days come, and numerous of them surfaced daily, she would look at me with tears in her eyes, and with a phenomenal strength which I assume came from above, she says, "Do what you do best." "God, You have once again managed to remind me that You are with me through Norah. God, just don't leave me, because You know if You leave, I will take the easy way out"…

It is two weeks since Wade's death, I wake up with either a sentence or a few words, and I'm writing it down and for some reason, dating them or typing them into my phone. Don't ask me why I'm doing this; I just have the need to keep these little sentences. When I'm at work, I would just go to where I keep all my little notes, and just add to the pile whatever I have received on that particular day. The day's turns to weeks then to months, and the little words and sentences are still coming. They are getting quite a lot. I still don't quite understand why I'm getting this, anyway the little notes or messages are not important right now, I need to deal with what is at hand, learning to cope and live without my boy, my reflection of life.

"When will I be able to close this box Lord, will this ever happen? Tell me Father, I have the right to know," I wipe the tears from my eyes. My arm slides across my nose. I don't want the person next to me in the taxi to see me cry, it's just that I want to do this privately. Turning my head I look through the window, the tears are rolling, and as they come, I wipe them away with my hand. Suddenly! I realize that I'm not ashamed to shed the tears. I want the world to see my agony; I want the children to see it too. They need to know what agony it is to live with, by the choice of suicide, and the impact they leave behind by those choices Lord. Oh Lord, help me Father; this is so raw and so painful. The thought scares me. The tears roll down my cheeks, little droplets drop onto my lap. If only I could hold them, cradle them, and look into them, perhaps they could reveal something.

This cruel fate has changed the course and direction of our lives, looking back I see . . .

CHAPTER 4

WADE ON THE WATERS

I now understand how Wade left us in front of the troubled waters. I step into the waters, what a waging war erupts; it's inside each of us, the battle that we are fighting daily, as a person, and family since Wade's suicide. Should suicide be an option? I drop to my knees and I call out to God to help me understand this, the war that wages. I look up to heavens, tears rolling, I cannot understand it. "How could this happen to me, to us? God tell me why, answer me father, a glimPse, an indication. I need to know God. Tell me, tell me please Father. Show me a sign so that I may know." Suddenly a sentence, a word or two, or three, would appear, I'm jotting them down again through teary eyes. "Take my heart God, and hold it for me until I am ready to take it back, for the pain that consumes this heart is so deep, that no man would ever be able to handle. Lord, every child should know that suicide should never be an option or even a consideration."

Demi's silence is deadly, she's not speaking, I can see the war that's waging within her, it wages continually. I'm waiting to see when this volcano will erupt; there is no closure to this chapter for my children. The war wages within Sheree, she is angry at the entire world. She no longer has a brother, she needs to understand why. She needs to understand how this happened, how she lost her only brother. No one can replace or give him back to her. It is too little, too soon for the sisters, on both sides. How long will this war wage within us.

Again a little sentence, and once again I jot it down. "Why these little sentences Lord, what help will they be to me? I don't need the sentences I need my son, my sanity and my life. Nothing can heal this gigantic hole within the heart and soul of the family. They will neither comfort, nor make us feel good. They just senseless little sentences."

The deadly silence has entered our homes and is here to stay. The emptiness and loneliness reigns in our lives now. I am angry at the world. I hate this world we live in. Life is meaningless. How do I continue to live on this earth, when my heart is with God and Wade? Demi knows me; she looks deep inside of me. She's read me; she walks away, then turns back to me and says, "You still have three other children you know." I look at her, does she know what is inside of me, does she know the war that wages within, does she have any idea of the darkness that surrounds me, I want to scream, but the words won't come out. I'm going crazy with the silence. Am I any good to her, Sheree or Niah? Am I any good here being like this? I'm dying and fading away. Is this what my girls and boys are supposed to see and live with? I look in the mirror, I don't see me, I only see pain. Joy is so far away, I can't reach it. I stretch out my hand to grab it, but in vain. Darkness has surrounded me. I look up to the heavens, "Lord, I only see pain and suffering." I call to God, "My God, how am I to walk when all I see is a tunnel of darkness filled with mud, rock and stone. There is no light only blackness, I need to find the light. Lord, help me to find the light."

The phone rings, and I'm brought back to the present. It's Sheree, she's crying, "Mummy I miss my brother, how could this be, how did this happen, how do we live without him? I had a dream and I was afraid, I called him, but he walked away from me mummy, and I could do nothing to stop him from leaving me. I tried to grab him but he just continued walking. I felt so helpless." We are crying, I put down the phone, walking to my bedroom, sitting on the end of the bed, the tears roll, she's opened the box without her knowing, the river starts flowing, my safe place, and my haven. Just then, Demi storms back into the room.

Suddenly . . .

THE VOLCANO ERUPTS

Before I can say anything it explodes . . . "He was my brother! you have no idea how hard it is for me to go to school! Do you know that when I wake up and I don't hear him, I want to go crazy! the quietness kills me!" Tears streaming down, "No-one sleeps next to me, wakes me up, no Wadey walking with me, no sharing or irritating me, no bringing me lunch at school." Gosh! She's looked into the box and touched that darn waters. It continues gushing out through the tears, "No Wadey at school, no hugs, kisses, no I love you, no do you know how beautiful you are, no if you weren't my sister I'll date you. We were only thirteen months apart, he was my other half." "Demi, I'm so sorry for this cross you, Sheree, Niah and everyone have to carry. Demi..." "No mom, leave me, it's my pain, I want to feel it, and I want to walk with it. You tell me that everything will be ok, but I know nothing will ever be ok for us."

What now Lord? Comfort is so far away for all . . .

Dropping to my knees, the only comfort I have is calling on God to help me, to strengthen me, without Him holding me, or my family, we are not going to make it. I don't want to think about it, "Help me Father, hold my heart and my family's heart in Your hands." I feel the pain eases, His calmness comes over me. I get up, I can do it, I can face another day.

Was this all too much for my little boy? so you leave . . .

THE EMPTY SPACE

And with that emptiness is a war within, and I know that when you open that box, the tear's that comes from it is so deep, deep within you. I see how you are trying to run through it, just like Jonathan in the bible with his sword. You fighting this battle within, and I fear that you are not going to see the end of this journey, "Stop! Jon. Stop, to think and feel, you cannot continue with this waging war. You need God's guidance. Dad needs God's guidance. I need God's guidance. Our children and family needs God's guidance," the empty space is slowly invading . . .

I refuse to go back and talk about the events on that fateful day, Tuesday the 24th May 2011, it just doesn't make sense, and leaves me in a state that I cannot comprehend and don't want to talk about, it's just too damn painful. What I will carry on writing about, is how the empty space starts invading my life after the tragedy.

Before starting my story, I would like to mention that eight months before Wade's tragic passing, I dreamt that Wade had died tragically. How? I'm not sure, but it was in some sort of accident. I woke up from that dream screaming and crying uncontrollably. My wife asked me what was going on, and with tears rolling down my face, and trembling, I told her that Wade had died. She called Venessa and told her what had just happened. She came over to my place, and my wife and Venessa had to comfort me, and sat with me until I eventually fell asleep.

What I should have done was to bind that dream and pray that it never happens, alas this I didn't do . . . gosh, I wish . . .

So my story begins . . .

A painful year has passed by without my Wadey by my side. I don't know how I've gotten so far, but I can only put it down to the grace of God. I sometimes wonder why Wade has never come to me in a dream, then something tells me, "In time Jon, in time," and tears would flow from my eyes. I sometimes think, "Why, Wadey, why?" and again tears roll from my eyes.

More months go by without my Wadey, and I just keep wondering why? And then the most unbelievable things start happening to me, Oh! No, suddenly, all these flashes start surfacing.

I'm driving along the R59 to Vereeniging, Wades face flashes in front of me, with that awesome and enduring smile, but in an instant it's gone. I scream, "Why! Wadey, why?" and then the tears start flowing down my cheeks. I sob uncontrollably, and then God reveals to me, as if in an instant, that all is well with Wadey. And yet, I can't control my grief and pain, but have to believe that all is well with him.

I'm so damn angry at God, then I ask myself, is it right to be angry with God? I think not, do I have the right to be angry with God? I think not, do I question God? I'm not sure. My mind plays all these games with me. I ask, "Why did Wade not talk to me if he was feeling so down? how could he just walk away from me after all we shared, and the surreal relationship we had? I cannot explain the bond we shared, because nobody will ever understand." "But Jesus, You knew and You understood, so why did this happen?" Again I become angry with God, but I don't have the right, or do I? I don't know yet. Will I ever know whether I have the right to be angry at You? Because as I . . . .

TAKE THIS WALK

The empty space next to me walks with me. The place where Wadey always was, and as I look back, I see my grandson Cael running and trying to catch up, and fill that space. But I don't allow it, because I'm entrapped in silence, just wondering why did Wade go away so abruptly, why did God allow this to happen? I then ask in a loud and screaming voice, "God! if You there, answer me!" And all I have is a deafening silence, and the pain starts all over again. I try to say, "Stop Jono, stop," but the pain in my heart, the pain in my mind, and the pain in my body, makes me shake, and then I sit down with my head bowed, and ask God for forgiveness and mercy, for not trusting in Him. And so my day and life goes on. Will tomorrow be any different? I don't know. Often I stare into the distance looking for . . .

CLARITY THROUGH

All this madness I'm going through. A deep need consumes me, wanting clarity and wanting it now. Will this ever happen? the 'clarity' to this entire mess, it does not come to me, but my heart is longing so dearly for it. Where is my boy? Where is Wade? or when will this ever change? . . . . then reality strikes, and I know that it will change, whenever I want it to change . . . . Gosh, I want it to change, and go back to Wade being alive, but that cannot, and never will be. Once again the tears just flows uncontrollably down my cheeks . . . . will this pain ever end? . . . . I don't know.

Days later, I am thinking deeply about what happened, and why, my anger then turns to Wade. "How in heavens name could you do this to me and our family?, you were going to be a superstar footballer." I am now only thinking about myself, to heck with everyone else . . . "I put so much effort into you Wade, I spent so many hours on the football field coaching you to be what you wanted to be . . . I spent so much time driving you up and down, from pillar to post to enhance your football career, I did everything you wanted from me, gave you everything you ask for, so how, and why did you do this to me? . . . nobody else . . . just me." I scream, "Damn you Wade! damn you! . . . You tell me Wadey, give me the insight into why? so that I can find that peace, that I so urgently, and desperately seek." All of a sudden, the anger subsides, and I see his smiling face, and hear him say, "You are my best Uncle, I loved you unconditionally and I am forever grateful for all you had done for me," screaming back at him, "Why then! Wade, why then?" . . . but only silence replies, the tears are once again shed and rolling uncontrollably . . . when will this end . . . when?

Lying, on my couch watching . . .

THE BEAUTIFUL GAME

These ordinary players playing professional football and I think that Wade could do all those things and more. The promise he made to me one day, he will play for Arsenal in the U.K and boy! Was he on track in my opinion. He could do things with a ball that you see Messi and Neymar of Barcelona do, and again the pain starts, and the tears well up in my eyes, and start rolling down. Boy! so many tears, where do you come from? and where do you go to?

Suddenly all those horrific thoughts surface and once again, I am tormented with the same scenario as to, Why! Wadey, Why! I then ask God again, "Why did this happen?" and again, the only answers I get to my questions, is just complete emptiness and silence, and in my mind, I again ask, "How long will this torment on the suicide of Wade carry on?" and once again, all the unanswered questions just hangs there in mid-air. Then that little voice again in me says, "As long as you want it to go on." Sitting up with all that is in me, I ask God, "Deliver me from this pain," and once again, the deafening silence is the only reply.

Thinking to myself, how I hate this game that I lived for and loved so much . . . . the game everybody calls, 'The Beautiful Game'. I close my eyes, and drift off into another world with tears again rolling down my face, and hope for some kind of peace of mind, as I see him scoring those beautiful and wonderful goals, the beautiful poise, and grace with the ball, the smile on his face, as always when he played, and the ultimate joy when he scored . . . . priceless. And how the people would say, "Who's that number eight?" Drifting into a deep sleep, and then waking up a few hours later back at square one, and all over, the torment would start again. "How long?" I ask, "How long?" . . . and once again, all the unanswered questions just hang in mid-air.

Weeks later, I would wake up in the morning, and my first thought would go to my Wadey. Such a wonderful, well mannered, good looking, and caring boy, who always gave and showed so much respect to his fellow players and elders. I enter into my bathroom look into the mirror, and the mirror stares back at me, and all I can see is the horrendous, and anguish look on my face. The pain is all over my face, I see how I have aged, how grey my hair has become, and how I am struggling to cope with the passing of my dear boy. Again the tears start to roll down my cheeks, and again I go into a stupor, and again I ask, "Why! Wadey, why!" Then again I question God, and I look for solace in the mirror, but all I see is my tormented face, and the torment starts all over again, and I wonder how long this is going to last, or will this go on. Is there no rest for my soul or my body, that has really taking a beating since Wadey's passing? I get dressed and leave for work to do my day's job, wondering why did this have to happen to me, my

whole family, and especially my sister. Screaming, in my car . . . .
"Why! why?" Punching the roof of my car out of desperation and
frustration, and so I try once again to get through another awful
day . . . . "God, when is the going to end . . . . when?" Once again
all the unanswered questions start unravelling just like a bird ruffles
his feathers. So wish I could just gather those ruffled feathers and
dump them where no one has to see them ever again . . . .

THIS SPACE, I HOLD

It will always remain empty, and through that, I will have to live
probably for the rest of my life on this damn freaking earth. The
space Wade left behind is such a huge space that I cannot even
comprehend anyone filling that space . . . . but I pray that perhaps
in time, God will find someone, or something to fill it, so that I
may be able to, sort of carry on with my life. Maybe one of my
grandsons Cael, Liam or Kylan will one day fill that empty space
that walks next to me. I dearly hope so.

But Wadey will always remain in my heart, body and soul for as
long as I live.

He was 'One of a kind, my kind' and so in realising this, I know
the space you hold, it will always remain empty, and through that,
I see it most clear how Wade . . . .

THE REFLECTION

. . . Of when you trap that ball, you look up for those empty spaces,
and running into it, I saw me, your grandfather. You became me in
the prime of my soccer career, my grandson, my feet.

I no longer see my feet in younger days. You were my image, my youth, I saw myself through you. Then you became my eyes in my old age, my hands on the steering wheel, and my eyes on the road. Then you left me, your feet have also left me, including your eyes and ears. Wade, you left me shattered and alone.

The anger I have from your death. My love for you ran deeper than you can imagine. I miss the phone calls from you, no smiling face, a hug, no watching you train. I studied you from the tender age of two. I would teach you a move and it would stay, and if you made a mistake, ten pushups and ten times around the house for punishment. You loved it, and I loved watching you, and the pleasure I found in it. Now, I have no one to talk to, to drive with or to watch train. What you gave back to me I can no longer see, because you no longer here. But what I miss most is just you, my grandson from my youth, I can no longer see my reflection in you, for the reflection of who I am is now in heaven.

And left behind is . . .

THE TRAGEDY

It grabs hold of me. I see how I'm sitting between the rubble, just like the 911 tragedy. As I turn to face in the furthest most distance, I see the family scattered between the rubble. The tears are everywhere Father; I see how it pushes through the rubble. I know exactly where it's coming from, it forms that river. I know where it's going, and that I've opened the memory box.

I haven't even started picking up the pieces of my shattered life. "Get up Venessa," "No, I don't want to go further," "walk through the rubble Venessa." "Why Lord? How can I Lord, it's difficult to even lift myself. You know my pain, how am I to walk through the rubble, some of them are huge stones. It will take me a life time to walk through this." "Turn around Venessa and look." "No, I don't want to see." "You have to do it Venessa." "Why? Lord why? all I'll see is broken stones, just as broken as my heart and soul." Slowly, as I turn, I am amazed to see what we've gone through already, the rubble we've crossed is endless. "Lord, did we walk this?" "Yes Venessa," and I see how my family slowly starts getting up. "Can't I just sit here Lord, it would be so easy." Doesn't anyone understand that I am angry at death, exhausted, from this cross that I carry? Death robbed me of a child, it left me shattered, torn and angered.

Hatred starts circling; I can see it's looking for a place to land. I know exactly where it's going. I'm afraid because I know deep down, I'm ready to grab it and hold it, and if I do it's going to destroy me. I never smile, how can I smile? "Lord, is this what I've become, reduced to this?" Looking at everything, I want to smash it. Life handed us a cruel blow, I need to vent my anger. Desperately, I want to lash out at everything and everyone. How can I go through this pain? I'm so tired of all the questions in my head and heart. Life is so difficult; somehow, somewhere through it all, I can hear the words, "be still." "Lord, how can I be still, this turmoil is a killer. Should any parent bury a child, especially a child with potential and a great future ahead, but more than that, a child full of love?"

I guess God only knows the answer, because it certainly does not make sense, and I certainly don't have any answers to these damn questions, that's killing me slowly inside. Does anyone have an idea of where I am? Tears streaming, "Don't look at me, don't say I'm so sorry, and don't say to me it will get better or easier. Give my son back to me; that would make it better and easier. Do you know that suicide visits me?" it would be so easy to end this. Besides the war that's waging, the anger that's destroying, the pain that is killing, "Do you have any idea what's in my mind? so don't tell me you understand." No one will ever understand. Only I know that the need to be with the child that is no longer here, is far greater than to be with those that are here.

These words will come to haunt me years later . . .

IT'S WAGING WITHIN US

And as I step in the water, I look into it, I see the anger and hatred. Dropping to my knees I'm hitting the water, over and over, it splashes onto my face, I'm soaked, my eyes are blurred by the water. Wiping, too exhausted by all this, I sit down. The tap has opened, tears pours out. I don't want to look at the box any longer. It reveals all the turmoil. It's there, the anger. I'm looking at everything and everybody. The anger in me is volatile. I'm a ticking time bomb. The anger is so rife, I feel it explode. I'm screaming, crying, and calling out to God, as I walk down the road. Not a care in the world if they see me like this. Life has gone on, but for me . . . "Tell me lord, tell me? How did this happen, only you have the right to give life and the right to take a life. Nobody else has that right." I get into the house, I'm screaming, "Why me! why us Lord? this is not fair; I served You earnestly and fervently, I try so hard to live according to Your word, why am I being tested, and for what reason was my loyalty and love not strong enough to sustain me and my family." I look around, I drop to my knees balling my eyes out, hitting the ground, and slowly I feel the warmth enveloping me, and my sobs starts easing. I feel how the anger starts leaving me. I'm holding my head again, "Don't take the anger from me Father, the anger helps me to manage each day." "You won't hear me through your anger." "But Lord, I have the right to the anger." "Put your hands together Venessa." "No! No! I want to fight this war." "I can fight it for you." Slowly the hands come together and the prayers start coming. I go into worshiping Him in song. The peace is once again all around me. "You here father, Your love is here too, please father don't leave me, if You leave me You know my intentions, please don't let me choose the other way out. I need to one day meet with You and Wadey, grant me the strength to go on."

I open my eyes, its 6.30am, Wade needs to be at Bidvest. I jump up, realization hits me . . . Wadey is no longer here. Tears fill my eyes, I know the box is full. It doesn't matter, the river is there, and it will hold my tears and the family's. I bury my face in the pillow, it comes gushing out, and as the tears roll, it is replaced with a great sense of loss and emptiness. I don't want to get out of bed; my heart is so heavy, and as the heaviness fills, so the load gets heavier to carry. This burden is too big and heavy to carry, I cannot lift myself. I pull the sheet over my head and close my eyes, allowing my emotions to take over. Millions of little tears rolls, it reminds me of my heart, that is in millions of pieces. "How the heck could this be? why is life so difficult Lord? I chose Your way, yet the suffering coming from those choices leaves me flabbergasted, and lost, I don't know for how long my heart will be able to continue with this pain, and not just stop beating." This would become a pattern that would stay with me. Saturday becomes the worst day of the journey that I would walk. The one thing I do know is that I would never change the choices I made when I chose to walk with God, but I do know that . . . .

Suicide has destroyed us; you robbed us of our gift, our child, only . . .

THE PICTURE FRAME

. . . Is left, death and silence follows me everywhere. I'm so tired of having them with me. They are a constant reminder of my pain. "God, take them away from me, I can't anymore, I can't take the pain and the stillness, I want the noise, give it back to me, it belongs to me." "But he is with me now." "I know Lord, but just one last chance is all I'm asking." Sitting in the lounge, the deadly silence is all around us, I can feel death in our home, looking at your picture in that darn picture frame. "You know what I'm thinking God, can You hear me?" "I know You are here, I know You can hear me. If You are listening, then You should know my thoughts and probably knew them long before I even thought of them. Why are You allowing me to go through this? Is the pain that I've endured thus far not sufficient? Why not take me from this, the anguish that our family is enduring is too much, can't I trade places, my life for Wadey's, so that I can give him back to his sisters, Dad, Jon, the family and friends, I would do it within a blink of an eye." But the picture in the picture frame is all that stares back at me. So I get up, taking the picture, holding it against my bosom, I weep profusely for my child. The deadly silence and the tears are all I know now. Cradling his photo, fingers rolling over his face, tears trickling down my cheeks, the little droplets drop onto his face, "I hope you can feel those tears Wade? and know the pain we live with constantly, without you by our side." I'm aware that I've touched the waters again and opened Pandora's Box to all the anguish.

Gosh! do you know . . .

THE MIRROR

. . . It's like the box; it reveals a lot, it's scary. I'm walking through the passage, a glimPse in the mirror, reveals just too much. "Is that me?" Gosh! this is just too much. Running into the bathroom, I feel the need to look again. Looking into that mirror, I don't see me, I only see pain, not just in me, but all around me. "No! No! No! this can't be." Dropping my head, tears rolling, I turn my head away, afraid of what I see in the mirror. "Look Venessa, look," "No, I can't, Lord, are You here?" Slowly, lifting and turning my head, looking through the corner of my eye, the mirror tells its own story. Dropping my head, tears drop into the basin, splashing into tiny pieces. It's a reflection of my heart, shattered into millions of pieces.

Goodness me, I've managed to unlock the box again. The reflection in the water is like the mirror, a true reflection of the chaos, the suffering, and the turmoil. Dropping to my knees, I cry out, "Wadey! Wadey, why did you leave me? How could you just walk away from me?" The person in the mirror can't be me. I need to get away. Getting up, turning, and running through the passage, I stop dead in my tracks; the mirror in the passage reveals the same reflection of what I have become. The pain, the loss, the anguish, but most of all, the loneliness and silence reflects. Tears streaming down my cheek, looking around, it's everywhere. "If he was not meant to be here, why did You give him to me?" just a glimPse of what could be? "What good is a glimPse Lord, if you can't have?"

Fear grips me, it's scary, and I can't bear to see or feel. Running out of the house into the street, I look at the house; it was his pride and joy. Now only loneliness and silence is like a coat of paint. My tears are rolling. I wipe them away, turning; I look down the road where Wade played street soccer with Jabu and friends. The silence in the road is even deadlier than the inside and the outside of the house. The quietness is deadly, looking and wiping the tears from my eyes, "Lord, death would be easier than living like this. This is a death sentence." Suddenly, I hear, "I'm so sorry Ma," turning around I see Jabu standing at the gate. Wiping the tears from his eyes, "How could he just leave us, I'm lonely without him Ma, he just walked away from me, leaving me alone, I miss him so much." "I know Jabu, I miss him too boy." "Why do You always do that Lord, You always find a way of sending little reminders to remind me that You always with me, so that I don't look for another way out. How can You love me so much, when I'm in so much turmoil?"

Turning back, I walk into the house. Where only silence, loneliness and . . .

CHAPTER 5

THE CHAOS

. . . reigns, did I ever think my life would take such a drastic turn of events? No, never, not in my wildest dreams. I would cry out to God to take me away, take me from this pain. If someone died, I would question God why that person, why not me. They are leaving behind everything, where as I have nothing to live for. Yes, I know I have other children and family, but right now it's not enough, I need Wade as well. "Don't You understand, that if I was no longer here, I would not feel and have to endure the pain and suffering, so why not take me, and spare me from this excruciating pain that is eating away at my heart and being. I keep telling You that I'm incomplete, and how do I live, and be a wife, a mother to my children and grandchildren, if I can't focus beyond this point. I have no reason or will to be part of this world. My entire world crumbled the day Wade died." I thought many times of suicide just not to feel that pain. Suicide stays in the back of my mind, as an option. But I would always have little reminders that would bring me back to the here and now . . .

Looking at the here and the now, is it worth looking at it. Everything is a mess, shear turmoil. I watch it crumble. Everything I worked towards in the world seems to be coming loose at the seams. "I need to mend this Lord; I need to find the grounding. Look at me, look at my life; look at our family, the chaos surrounds us." Slowly I see how everything falls apart. I'm trying so desperately to hold it together, but how? when I'm lost in this world, I no longer fit in here. "Will I ever have the need to fit in again," I wonder?

This wondering will walk this journey with me constantly. The only thing that stays constant in all this chaos is our relationship with God. "How can this be Lord, that the bond with You is getting stronger yet everything around us has started spiraling? I have to hold on to You Lord. Sometimes, no most times I fall, even though I don't know how, You lift me up. I know that to try and hold it together, I will need Your grace, because before I know it, I'm dusting myself off and I'm trying to take a step forward."

There are times when I can walk beside Jesus, and feel like running ahead of Jesus, and as I start running, I stop dead in my tracks and I turn back to look at Jesus, and I know that I can't do this without Him by my side. So I turn back and wait for my Jesus. There's those days when I lag behind, and can no longer hold onto the hem of His garment, and I want to let go and give up, then He stops dead in His tracks, and this time, He turns around and waits for me. So through the mess I know I can rely on Jesus to be there for me. What would happen if He was not there for me? I don't even want to touch those waters to reveal anything. I cannot handle the thought of that, so I leave the box unopened for now. I'm just so angry.

You left a rip in us . . .

From that rip so much of . . .

THE HATRED

. . . Within me. I hate feeling like this. You are no longer circling around; I've definitely managed to grab hold of you, as if I don't have enough handle. I've decided to take you on as well. Of course, silly me, did I think I can run from you. All the hatred is within me. The hatred of what life has handed me, the cards that was dealt, and the cruel fate of what lies ahead. I hate this with all my heart, I know God You never intended this. But the knowledge of not knowing is what's killing, like cancer that eats away at you. How could this happen to me? the emptiness within me is so riveting.

Watching soccer or seeing little boys play street soccer or riding down the road on their bicycles, it is just so . . . I look at clothing, I imagine you in it. Everywhere, there is a reminder of what could have been. I can't handle this. Living with this is just too hard. My life has become staggered, stop, start. No beginning, when I think of starting, little reminders surface, suddenly everything stops. Trying to start again, is so difficult, If only I could take you and throw you so far away where you have no way to return.

If I could walk away from this and from these feelings, perhaps then life could start and somewhere along the line, I could live a normal life. Will my life ever become normal? How long will I feel like this? I cannot live a pretentious life, it has to be real. Pretending everything is fine, when it's in such a mess, it would be a lie; God does not live by lies. You have to guide me, give me an indication. Living with a suicide is very difficult. I need to make closure and not look for another way out, without hatred.

Lord, how do I do this . . . ?

LIVING WITHOUT WADE

Life is strange, learning to live without a child. When you are young and you are starting out in life, you are afraid to bring them into the world and you wonder if you will cope. Then, as they come, you take snap shots of each child; you label each box, and leave it imprinted into your heart forever. Suddenly it's like it's been ripped out and you have to start learning how to cope, and live without the box that holds the snapshot to that child's life. Wade left such a huge imprint in my heart and in many others. In his walk, he taught us how to love unconditionally and openly. His humbleness and free spirit made life seem so simple.

My prayers have become harder and deeper, I look for relief within. If only I could take my heart, hold it and comfort it, perhaps the sense of this loss would vanish, it could be erased, but I know that is impossible. I know I have to take this journey of the unknown and carry the open book with me, so my prayers will never stop as long as I breathe, as this heart beats and the blood pumps through it, and as I grasp for that one last breath, I shall hold onto Your garment, the box, and the book, until I no longer can. I shall call to You my Father, for the grace that I may walk in Your footsteps forever. Help me to find that peace each day as I open my eyes, and help me that when I close them, and lay my head down, I shall find rest until I open them for a new day.

Often I wonder . . .

WHERE DO I GO FROM HERE

"Only You God can tell me where I go from here. Yet, You insist that I open the box. Is the agony and pain within not enough for You? You want me go through it." Tears rolling, I touch the memories in that box again, damn it; you will always be there . . . the reminder that my life is on hold. With my fingertips touching the memories, emotions surges through me, flashbacks comes to the fore, "Wadey, Wadey why? you were my life." Oh! how I wish I could just erase the last three years.

Questions start rising to the surface in the water. Gosh! they floating all over, but looking further back I see you there, something scary. I'm not ready to handle you yet. So I'll leave you

in the back there, because I know you will always be there . . .
but the one that stands out and is most pertinent for now is, what
could I have changed that March after Wade got sick? What was I
supposed to change? "Father, help me, and tell me Father, so that
I can understand and resolve it all." Most fathers always have the
answers for their little girls, because without those answers life is
just so difficult to live. Why would a child take his or her life and
leave behind so much pain and suffering, but most of all, the mess,
and the chaos that is left behind after a suicide, is unbearable.

You never intended pain for Your children, only love and happiness.
God, You have to help me, help me please, to accept the reality.
I need to hold him Lord, to touch him, to see him grow, to feel
that hug, to hear him whisper in my ear, "I love you mom." "You
loved me more, but do you know that I loved you most Wadey . . .
more than life itself." Lord, could You not have taken me instead
of Wadey? I would do anything if I could trade places, my life for
Wade's. I've lived my life. I'd wake up with this awful feeling, a
feeling of immense loss, that my child's not coming back and that
I need to know why, and how long I must live with these feelings?
I need to find a way, but I just don't know how. With the very
strength I slam the box to hide the hurt, unbearable pain surges
through my being, holding my chest,

I weep for my boy and once again . . .

CHAPTER 6

THE LITTLE SENTENCES

. . . Appear. Cradled on the floor and through my tears, the little sentences come. I don't know why, but I'm typing them into my cellphone, sitting on the floor. Should I get up, or should I just rather peep into the box, and look at what is in store for me? Suddenly like a flash of lightning, the thought comes to mind . . . why don't you put it together Venessa, I shrug at the idea. Why are these little words or sentences rolling in? I don't understand. Why I am even writing them down? but for some reason I do.

Its two weeks before Wade's first anniversary and a cloud of emotions hangs over us, I can feel it, the pain, the sense of loss, the devastation, I need my Wadey. Help me to find a way of working through it. The thought occurs again, and the little words and sentences, I know God, You want me to finally put it together. And so I start piecing them together to my amazement it was actually a letter that was written from my inner most being.

But I think perhaps God had a hand in it . . .

THE LETTER

DID GOD DEPICT OUR JOURNEY

To: Wade Devin Mulligan-Adams

Today I write this letter to you Wadey my boy, you walked away from us a year ago today but it seems like yesterday. This is so much harder than the day it happened. When your life ended, you took our lives too, and put the candle of light out in our hearts. The road you have chosen and that you lay before us is the most difficult road for any person to walk. You chose a road of destruction. You left behind total chaos. You ripped our hearts out and left it scattered. We sit among the rubble; tears rolling from all directions, a river forms. I look into it, I see pain and suffering. We sit in awe, waiting and wanting.

I call upon God, but I feel the deadly silence ripping through my heart. We're alone, lost and lonely. We sit trying to piece it together. I asked God for a needle and cotton to mend it, but the pieces are so tiny, all we see is stitches. I asked God for glue but it sticks to our fingers. Our hearts are torn into pieces. We have not picked up any pieces of our shattered hearts. I watch in silence as we fade away slowly.

Again, I call upon God to lift us, He tries so desperately. The weight God carries because of our loss is unbearable, so imagine how it is for us boy. I'm ready to tip, but God grabs me. We reach out for you, and God gives us His hand. We cry for you, and God wipes our tears. I cry out to God for help, and He puts out his hand, I'm hoping for yours. We know you are safe, but we are far from that. We fall, and God lifts us, and that is how we've walked this year.

A thought in our minds, a memory in our hearts, Oh! how I wish you would rather be a laugh we could hear, a smile we could see, a hug we could feel, a brother, a son, a grandchild, a cousin or uncle we could hold. I would never let you go not for one minute even to breathe. I reach out, I call, I search, but in vain you are only but a picture in a picture frame.

You left a void, an unbearable emptiness that cannot be filled. You ripped the safety net under us, but in the process you taught us that God is and will always be supreme and through that lesson we have learnt to lean on God and no longer on you.

But if God asked us if there was anything we would want to change in our lives, the one thing we would never change are our children, they are a gift from God, special and unique in their own way. Each one has a significant meaning in our lives that completes the circle of life and I would choose you again, and again, even if only for fifteen years.

After reading the letter, I now know that God had predicted . . .

THE ROAD AHEAD

Actually, I know that every message I received, was a message from God. Two weeks before Wade's second anniversary, on the 9 May 2013, God revealed to me the actual meaning to the poem. God revealed that, the messages He had given me in the letter would depict the journey, not only I would walk after Wade's death, but my entire family, and that I should go and read the letter.

I read the letter, but only after the fourth time, since writing it, I looked at the letter with a spiritual eye, and for the first time I could actually see the road my family and I are on, and in my revelation, God opened my eyes, and what I saw was . . . devastating! And as I turned back to look, I see how our entire family is actually sitting among the rubble just like the 911 tragedy, and in the furthest distance, I see myself sitting and not going anywhere. For me death has replaced life, presence just exists, future has disappeared, happiness has been replaced with sadness, dreams have faded, life has ended through the choice of 'Suicide'.

Can I walk this road? I'm not too sure, but I do know that . . .

A MOTHER'S LOVE

. . . Is supreme, we should always remember that the tie, which links mother and child is of such pure and immaculate strength, it should never be violated. You, as a mother, are never really alone in your thoughts. A mother always thinks twice, once for her child and once for herself. A mother never ever considers giving up her child, and making the decision to have a child is momentous. It is a decision forever to have your heart walking outside of you, for a mother her love is instinctual, unconditional and forever. So in choosing death, you are actually taking the life of the person who brought you into the world, and the family.

Just remember every child is unique and special in their own way, and as children, they complete the circle of life in a mothers heart. If one link is missing, the heart is incomplete forever, and nothing will ever be able to replace that missing piece. You make a permanent solution out of a temporary situation. How permanent that impacts, is that as a parent we will never see them grow, matriculate, have a matric ball, become a professional, get engaged, marry and have children. Just remember that when you lose a child, you lose the future, and with a choice like 'Suicide' You leave behind a devastation that brings about chaos, total chaos!

So as a mother her . . .

HER STRENGTH

. . . Is phenomenal, you realize this through the tests.

Norah had a purpose to be in my life at that time, she taught me how strong I really am and can be in the sight of the Lord, even in my darkest time. Someone less spiritual than me, or so I thought, taught and showed me how God, Jesus and the Holy Spirit (The Trinity) works. He works through the less privileged, the less spiritual, and through that comes mighty works of God. I would come to see how, through my spirituality and strength, how God would work for me, and through me. The strength that I have is strength that was given to me from above. And through that Jesus says that . . .

GOING THROUGH THE WATERS

We know that our journey has only begun. I go under, opening my eyes I look around, twirling, I finally have a chance to look at everything around me. I want to take it all in before I surface. I want to see the chaos and the devastation that is in the waters. I need to keep it close to me; I need to take it with me through the waters. I don't want anyone to go through this ever again in this life time.

Once we have gone through the waters, will we be made whole? I have to believe this, that all will be right. Maybe not now but perhaps one day, I pray that my family will find the peace, even if my journey never comes to that. As long as they can once again smile, feel the peace, and be able to live again, and be made whole. Me, I'm not afraid anymore of the sadness, the loneliness, the loss, I can walk this alone God, because I made the promise, that this is between You and I.

So with Your strength, I will continually seek and with the knowledge that . . .

THE BOOK

. . . Will go with me as we begin a journey of the 'Unknown'. This becomes a journey that we walk in a world where only pain exists. No words or hugs can heal a parent's heart, a sibling's pain, or make a thought or wish come true. It's an unclosed chapter in our lives that we, at any stage of our lives, will never be able to turn a page, go to another chapter, or close the book. This book is left opened and unanswered forever. We walk with this book open until we close our eyes and go home to meet them. The one thing I know is that suicide is not an option, it's a devastation that leaves behind total chaos. But the one thing that becomes apparent while submerged is that, the tears are a permanent part of our journey, and the box is like the book, it will always remain open . . .

And so we go onto . . .

THE 'UNKNOWN'

Through the tears, the chaos and the devastation, I see how we walk the road of the 'Unknown' it is very difficult, anger and turmoil is everywhere as we step onto that road. The desert has become our home, and most times I have to stop and turn, to look for my children and family. I see in the distance, how they linger behind. God's grace has carried me; so I stop to wait for them. When I turn to continue, suddenly a huge rock is in front of me, the pain is back, the longing, and the need is there. I look ahead, I see nothing. Nothingness has come to play a very important part in my life. I see how my family leaves me behind and continue on their journey. I stand in front of the rock and I know I have to climb it to get across.

"Lord, can I do this, I can't anymore. I don't want to do this any longer. Boy! This mountain is huge, will I reach the top Lord? Don't let me go through this, I will not make it. How many mountains, rivers, dark tunnels, muddy and rocky ground will I have to go through before the pain will ease or go away? Tell me Father, because at this rate, I'm not going to ever be able to go through it, or start over," but amazingly, He gives me the strength as always, to continue this journey. Bracing myself for what lies ahead, bravely I start the climbing, though the tears, agonizing pain, the loss, the emptiness and the silence, makes it very difficult for me to reach the top. Eventually after much perseverance, I'm standing on the top of the mountain. This was too much for me, I'm ready to fall; taking that step would be easier. Taking this leap would ease the pain within.

The trail of the yellow pills is revealed in the waters. I've opened that damn box, it flows again, but I know God is here, I feel the hand on my shoulder. It hurts, Lord, so badly, this would be easier.

Sitting down, head in my hands, I allow the inevitable to happen. The tears stream down my face, I see how it runs all the way down the mountain, it just keeps rolling, I'm watching and wondering, where it's going, as it rolls in front of me in the distance. Jesus walks ahead of me or perhaps He waits for me to meet Him and . . .

So the unknown begins . . .

Will we finally be able to close this box? I don't know, but I do know that the water will continue to seep through the crevices. I decide to open the box for one last look, but that's ok, as long as I can close it, I'm thinking. I put my hands in the waters, gliding it through the waters; I see the picture rising to the surface, the vision is revealed. I watch in awe, how it runs and joins Wade on the waters, if only, we can go through it, our journey will become easier.

Another question that would end up walking with me . . . Only later would I realize you never close this chapter of the book, or the memory box, after a suicide in your entire life.

Had You prepared me thirteen years early for this . . . ?

CHAPTER 7

OH! LORD

"Tell me? did You prepare me?" "Should I show you more? do you believe I was there for you," "I don't understand why Lord?" "Do you remember the sea", "The sea? what about the sea," all at once the picture.

"No! No! No! You letting me go back to the box, Lord, why am I opening it, I thought we were finished." "Open it Venessa." "The water is here, You allowing me to walk along the side of the sea." I'm in the box again whether I like it or not. I'm on the beach; the children are playing all around. I wonder off, "You look so peaceful." Will I experience that peace? Oh! Lord I need that peace. "Looking at you it's so tempting everything will be erased." I stop, I look across the sea, it's never ending, but this would be a perfect ending to my misery. "Lord, You opened that box, the box I'm thinking of taking with me, You testing me Father," "No Venessa, I'm reminding you." "You are reminding me of what?" "I want to remind you that I was, and am always with you." "But I want to forget the beach and sea; it has so much sadness and pain, walking that beach without him is hard, he loved the beach."

The tears are there again, looking at the sea, it is so appealing. Taking one step, two steps, three steps, I stop, looking into the further most distance, it's so beautiful, peaceful and free. That freeness is what I need, free from everything. "Wadey, Oh! Wadey, you left me behind. I'm struggling boy, this would be easier. You told me you'd come back for me. I'm here boy, I'm here." "Lord, please allow me this freedom to walk. I'm broken, lost; the only thing that keeps me here is your strength." This time the tears roll down my face, drop for drop into the sea, if only the sea could wash it all away. "I told you I'm weak, only my faith is not weak. I'm broken, torn into pieces. I want to put them back together, but how Lord?" Dropping to my knees, the sea water washes me, this time I allow it to flow openly with no shame. It somehow eases the pain in my heart. As I wipe the tears, I hear, "Mummy! Nanna! come, we are looking for you." I hear my little brats, the smiles, the excitement to see me, and I know that You know what I'm contemplating. You've looked once again deep into me and You knew my intentions.

You knew Lord, that's why You sent them. Niah looks at me, she sees my tear stained face, she's like Demi, she knows my heart.

"You miss Wadey, Hey! Mom," "Yes girl," "You will be ok." She walks towards me put her arms around my neck, and says, "Don't worry, everything will be ok Mummy, Wadey still loves you, we love you and Jesus loves you more." Leaving a kiss on my cheek, she jumps up and runs to join her nephews. So much love around me, yet I'm lost.

"You sent them Lord," "Yes Venessa, through all your dark times was I not there, when you called? was I not there when your heart was too laden, and you asked me to take it, and hold it, did I not? Look back and see." I turn, suddenly I hear "Mummy! Nanna! Come! Come! Nanna! We need you." A Scary thought, "What would I have done had I not had You in my life." "But, I've always been there and will always be." Bended knees weeping, "Oh! Lord Oh! Lord, You really are here. I'm so sorry for all those ugly thoughts, all the doubt, please forgive me."

As for all your questions, a time and a place, but . . .

THE VISION I LONGED FOR

. . . Probably will remain with me and through my grieving. The need to hear from God and Wade, regarding the turmoil we were left in, grew deeper. I would pray for some revelation or vision, into what transpired on that day, or an encounter with the Trinity as to why? but looking back at my experiences in the last three years, I now realize that God had given me a much deeper insight into how He works. Probably the need for knowing, and the need for an encounter, or a dream, will always linger, but I have learnt that His love, understanding and patience, and most of all the wisdom that He gave to me in this walk, is sufficient for now. Looking back, I can see through the chaos He showed me, that what I prayed for was a far more spectacular encounter and vision than anyone can imagine in this life time.

We have no idea where we go from here, all we know is that we have found God's grace in this moment and time of our lives, and for us this is most important. Through Wade's death I have learnt to walk in Jesus footsteps. I realize by God allowing me to go through all this chaos, that though suicide no longer visits me, it will always linger, and though the pain grows deeper for the loss of my son, so does the love and the need grow even deeper for my God, my Jesus and Holy Spirit, and the need to know them, deeper and more intimate.

But . . .

The loss . . . .

The tears . . .

And the pain . . .

Will probably stay forever in . . .

THIS BROKEN HEART

Glancing into it, I see how Wadey picks up the pieces of my heart, holding it in his hands. Immediately I know what you revealing to me. I am not ready to let go of my boy, yes it's true, Wadey is holding my heart and that's where it will stay. "No God, it belongs to You and Wadey." I probably will never be able to release Wade, as for my heart, hold it until I can take it from You personally.

And as the day's turns to weeks, then to months and years, I do know without a shadow of a doubt that my heart will always belong to God and Wade.

And through . . .

THE ALPHA COURSE

. . . gave me a greater in depth into Jesus and His life. But what was even more amazing was that through this course I found out about . . .

THE GRIEF SHARE COURSE

Mildred, the grief share coordinator, came to speak about the course briefly after we completed the Alpha course. I'm thinking that I would like to be part of this, assisting people in their grief. Pushing it aside for now, I have to first learn to deal my grief before I can assist anyone else with theirs.

A few months later I received a mail from Yvonne Guest, our Alpha coordinator, inviting me to attend a grief share. Well, it's just for one day, so I accept and invite the family, sending a sms to my entire family inviting them to join me on the Saturday morning. For some reason only Dad and Jonathan confirmed, so off we went, arriving at the meeting we discover that it was a fourteen week course. Jonathan turns to look at me, I know what he is thinking, he can't make it. I'm not ready for this; I don't want to tell strangers about my inner feeling and fear. They won't understand this, they probably going to look at me and judge my son. Ok, so I'm here let me make the most of it, but I'm definitely not coming back next week.

The next Saturday I'm there, to my surprise, and the following Saturday. The third Saturday into the course, Jonathan says, "Nes, I don't know if I'll be able to handle this." I have to be strong, Jon is falling apart and Dad is still in his silence mode.

Suddenly seven weeks into the course, Jon is on the up, Dad has started opening up and I hit a downward spiral. Boy, I'm spiraling at an alarming rate, it's opening all these wounds, and this is not going to happen. I'm not going to allow myself to go back to that day, for a third time. The first was 'Wade's death,' and then 'the book,' and now Grief Share. I want to walk away, but for some reason I just can't. "I know Lord, You know what happening."

If only Jon, Dad and the entire grief share knew where I'm heading and that suicide was circling again. I'm so teary lately, a song, a word, a look, but mostly a song would open the tear duct, and it would flow uncontrollably. No stopping this, as it drops; I see how it rolls to the box. This feeling never left until the twelfth week into the course.

Through the teaching I felt the burden lift slowly; suicide is not circling any longer. I've managed to keep it under control. By the fourteenth week I'm on an upward and with the closing, Myrtle comes over to me and says, "Venessa, I was so concerned, I saw the suicide tendencies. But I'm amazed you back to looking like the first day you walked in."

We came to walk an amazing journey of pain, loss, anger and disappointment, but through that we discovered the sincerity of love. The maze of suffering we walked together holding onto each other for strength, seeking comfort, helping in carrying the cross, when it became too heavy to carry alone.

Oh! Yes, there were times when we fell along the way side, but there always seemed to be someone there to pick up the cross and walk it with us until we were strong enough once again, and could carry it alone.

It became an amazing fourteen week journey that would take us through all our fears, the anger, the hatred, the sense of loss, helping us to work through our grief, and to cope overall. For the first time since Wade's death, I felt and understood everything that was within me. It taught us how handle and work through our situations step by step. But what captured me mostly was that I knew I was no longer alone in a world where only pain existed, I had people who understood and were walking exactly the same road in a different way. I was no longer afraid to face my fears that I carried within. I could openly express it through the tears, the grief and the anger.

Grief Share is over, our anchor is gone, even Niah feels it, "Mom can't we go back? I feel safe when we are at grief share." Suddenly I'm sinking, Oh! No, I'm back in the box; I need to get away from it, but for some reason I'm looking into it. Gosh! you there again, as clear as day light, the laughter, the dreams, the loss, the fear, the pain, the tears, the anger, the trusting, and lastly the answers that will never be revealed.

They are all surfacing. I see how I stretch out my hand; it's in the waters, I'm touching them one by one. They move from the fingers through to the arm. It enters the heart, the pain is there again, I'm shivering, the tears are welling up in the eyes, slowly they drop and from that comes the reality that we cannot hold onto anyone or anything for comfort, only God.

"Why did I do that? Why did I start trusting man, and drift away from trusting only You." Turning away from the box, through the tears, I'm saying to God, "If only the tears were laughter, If only the dreams could come true. If only the prayers were answered. If only I could have it, I would steal every laugh, every dream, every answer and every trusting, it would be a moment I would treasure."

The way you were, you made us shine. Knowing that I cannot have it, I call to God bowing my head, and out comes . . .

THE PRAYING HANDS

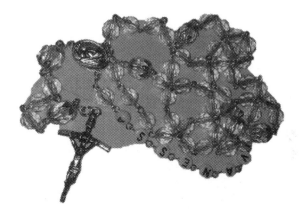

And as the days appear, so does the rosary, and with that comes the kneeling and bowing of my head in prayer. "Father, don't let anyone ever again have to endure this pain. Help me to find a way to stop this. The suffering as a mother, father, grandfather, uncle, aunt, sister, nephew, cousin, has been so severe through this suicide. Nothing in my life right now is worth living. The struggle daily to wake up and go on, is beyond any understanding, there is no way of knowing whether we will one day be able to pick up all the broken pieces, move on, and live a normal life." Closing my eyes, I feel the enormous loss within. "All I know is to reach out and call out for Your help, and in my prayers to You; Father, is that no one should ever endure this pain. Please help me in a way to stop 'Suicide'. I would never want anyone else to feel this way, but if they should go through it, I pray, that they at least have You in their lives to cope with this tremendous loss, because I certainly don't know how I would do it, if I did not have Your grace on me and my family."

This will become a priority, and will play an integral part of the journey that we must walk. So, as I tell the story, the longing for my boy goes far beyond this earth and extends to the heavens with God and Wade, and as I look back, I see my three girls, and I know I have to go back and complete what God has set out before me . . .

My head bowed, "Lord, this road is the hardest to walk. The steps are tiny ones, delicate with a tear drop to every step, with a deeper need for clarity to understand it all, but most of all to find the inner peace that will wrap itself around this wounded heart, and make it whole again." Could a mother's love run any deeper? Yes, to the ends of the earth and beyond. Deep within me, my prayers are that perhaps one day, we can close this box for good, seeing that most of the tears are now in the river. I know that the book though will remain open.

My wait is patient, as my journey continues I see . . .

CHAPTER 8

THE WISHES

To: my brother Wadey

I love you, and I wish you were home,
It hurts me to think you're so alone.
It's not the same without you here,
Why you did what you did, is still unclear.
I remember when you were little
and played in the yard,
Then you'd go sit inside and watch Pokémon!
You'd look at me and smile,
Your smile use to stretch a mile.
When I had a bad day you were the only one
Who could make me laugh?
It's like you were my other half.
It hurts me to see you gone
It hurts even more because
there's nothing I can do.
I just wish I could make it all ok,
But all I can do is pray.
I pray for you every night before I go to sleep,
And every time I think I hear you creep
I break down and weep.

Sometimes it's like you're still here,
I look at the door and wait for you to appear.
Then I realize you're not coming back!
And I go back to feeling so alone.
I love you so much you just don't know,
I'm at my breaking point, at my lowest of low
Even though you in heaven so safe and sound,
I wish you were here with me.
So that I can tell you every day that
You're my brother and I love you!

Your sister
Sheree

Hi Wadey,

How are you, mum she's fine. I
hope you fine. Yes I'm fine.
This is my journey after your
death Wadey. I have shed
A lot of tears. My heart is broken
and I am very sad. I
See you often. Mom says I must tell you she loves you
Most and says we love you more.
She cries a lot Wadey, she misses u so much.

Yes!! Wadey when will you tell me why you died.
I miss you my only brother forever and ever.

Love You

Your sister
Niah

Wadeo,

Bless us Lord as we pray you took
our little boy home to stay.
Please let him know
Please as we pray
How much we
Loved him every day
We loved his laugh
We loved his smile
We loved his everything
We loved our child

Bronny

Wade Devon Mulligan you were
born into this family
And everyone was just so happy,
Venessa having a son
I looked after you for three year
when you were little
Sometimes you gave me hell never
wanted to polish your shoes
Never wanted tomato gravy over your
pap instead milk and sugar
And when you were really naughty I'll
wait till you in the bath sneak in
With the scissors to cut your willy, as you grew
into this well-mannered and beautiful boy
You just stole everyone's heart and gained
all the respect from millions of people.
There's so much more I can write about you . . . .
After Cass died you crept deeper into my life
and heart, my visits twice a week before soccer

Emails from BBM, sitting on the chair
next to me on your phone sipping
your coffee we made together
Good and special memories I have
of you . . . . just so sad.

Wade Devon Mulligan

He said goodbye and walked away just yesterday
And then we just let him go
He went to Church the night before
We never said we love you so
We went to work and then we got the call
Could we please come your son is gone
Something has happened and it's grave
We cannot save his life

No, we never said goodbye and
we never really told him
Just how much he meant to us
No, we never said goodbye, now it's too late
And he's just a memory
How can we go on?
Now that his gone

We will know, until we die
We never said goodbye

His perfume lingers all around us now
A pair of shoes lies on the floor
The bed made up where just last night he laid
We cannot say we close the door
A list of dreams he'll never have
Photo's hanging on the walls
Is that his laugh I hear out in the room?
We turned and call, but he's not there

No, we never said goodbye and
we never really told him
Just how much he meant to us
No, we never said goodbye, now it's too late
And he's just a memory
How can we go on?
Now that his gone
We will know, until we die
We never said goodbye

You're Aunty
Lin

I loved you unconditionally

My uncle . . .

"I so wish my uncle was still with us"
What are we going to do without him?
He won't be able to see us grow up,
And Kiyaan won't even know him at all!

If God gave me only one wish,
I would wish you back,
To kick ball with me,
To surf with me but most of all
Just to hold us.

It's not fair that I don't have my uncle here.

Tashreeq

Hey mommy, bring me a spade quickly,
I want to dig Wadey up out of the ground
So that he can come play soccer with me.

Niyaaz

What is life after my brother Wadey

Josh: You never cease to tell me that, it makes me think of Wade. He was my pillar, to be honest; I have not taken one step forward since he died. I'm stuck and I can't find my way forward. No one will ever know what I'm going through. My family thinks that they suffering alone, and they never take me into consideration. I'm so lost, I don't want to wake up every morning but I do, and fight my pain because I think of my mother. If I feel so lost and heartbroken, how does she feel? There are days when I get so frustrated with the fact that he's gone that I have to sit, try and calm down in order to regain myself. I dreamt of him last night, I was fighting the ends of the earth to get to him but before I can get through, he's gone. how do I find myself, he was my brother, best friend and everything a girl can ask for in a brother. And all because people were jealous, because of unknown reasons, I had to lose him. I didn't ask for him to be taken away and yet he was. I don't think it's fair. I've never been so sad. My whole family mourns yet I find myself alone stuck among the 911 rubble with no one to turn to, but to endure every bit of pain and suffering I'm feeling.

Demi: You're right, no one will ever know how your pain feels. But I can tell you there are people that love you and care about you, would take the pain from you if they could, I know I would. But we won't know. The amazing thing is you have so many people caring about you and that loves you. You need to accept that we are here for you. Not just one but many people who's there for you. You aren't stuck in life Demi, Your heart is sore and you have every right to be. We are here for you and your family loves you. No one knows what goes on in your heart and life but trust me we want to make it ok. If it means me been the only one that loves and care about You I will be. I really wish I could take the pain away from You Demi, but Your strong, You so strong Demi and God is with You, trust me. Stay faithful to him and believe in Him and with that believe in yourself. Your life will endure through this, your life will grow. Just continue with your beliefs. Live your dreams for Wade. Do great for Wade.

Your friend,
Josh

- - - - - - - - -

Wadey Boi

We became friends in grade one at TC Esterhuysen Primary school. You took me under your wing and became my best friend. I started playing soccer with you under eight for Gorretti football

Club. Nothing could separate us. When you moved over to Florida Albion Grandpa said I needed to be there as well, so off I went and joined you. You went to JSS high school and of course I had to follow. We became the formidable two. You would ensure that Grandpa picked me up for school, and dropped me as well. You looked after me and I spent all my life training, and being with you, Uncle Jon and Grandpa all that time. What an amazing life that would have become. Then you left me torn and tattered. I often think of you and miss you more than you could ever imagine. I feel like I lost a part of me. You were more like a brother. Words can't explain what you meant to me. Even thou you no longer with us, we still a team. Life is not always what it seems to be. I reminisce every day about the good, and bad times we had, you can't imagine the pain I felt. I know that you are living your life after death, in the future I hope that you will open up that gate of heaven for me.

Love you always

Your brother

Tshepo

*A talented Young football star/
player the world had lost.
R.I.P my good South African
Friend Wade Mulligan*

My brother Wade

*Since the day we met I knew things were never
going to be normal between us, because from the
start we just had an instant connection as if we
were never friends in the first place but meant
to be brothers. We did everything together, went
everywhere together and never kept anything from
each other. I could swear we were separated at
birth, because there was nothing that we both love
or hate. The whole plan was that we would both
become these famous soccer players and would
buy the biggest house and live together. When we
were together it was like nothing could go wrong.*

We went to our first high school party together,
taking him to Park Town Girls with his
grandfather's hat on that night was so funny
and being around him, he would always for
some reason find a way to pull his pants down
and walk around without his pants on.
I never thought that I would never see our dream
come true together and the day I got the news it
felt like an entire half of me was ripped away.

But I do know he will always be watching over
me and looking after me as he always did.

Love u Wade

Joshua

Matthew Pelton Your Bidvest Buddy/ brother,

I just want you to know coming from Cape Town
to Joburg, a new city and life. I missed my family
and realising that I needed to do this on my
own. I met a Young boy whose name was Wade
Mulligan at Bidvest. The first day Wade came to
training he asked if I was the boy from Cape Town,
from that we started a friendship that turned to
brotherhood. Wade took me under his wing and
that's how we became friends. He brought me
home into his home every other weekend. I was
amazed at the kind of family Wade had they were
very loving, caring, and joy filled their home.

As our friendship continued I became his brother
"his boeta" the older brother. Wade was an
extremely jolly, loving and caring person, I never
heard him ever complain. The one thing Wade

taught me was never to be shy to ask for anything.
Something we were taught at home never to do.

There are so many times I would just sit thinking
about him, how awesome he was and the times we
shared I treasured most. We were truly best friends
or best brothers forever until one day he just left us
all in shock and pain which happened so fast. Our
lives were all of a sudden empty because he was no
longer there to continue with us. I never thought
that even though his no longer here it feels as
though his still here with me. He has risen to be
an angel and will always remain in our hearts,
mind and soul. It took me a long time to release
him to rest but up till now I can't believe his gone.
I thank God for letting him come into my life and
allowing me to come into his life and his family.

Thank You Wade for coming into my life, my
brother I will never forget you, nor my family.
May you rest in peace my brother I love you.

Matthew.

Aunty Nessa,

Often when I watch soccer, no one's comes close
to Wade. He was unique. He would have been one
of the greatest soccer players with a style of his
own. I have never seen anyone come close to the
talent of Wade, perhaps Europe's greatest, but for
me Wade topped that and more. To watch him
Play was just awesome, the boy and friend with
a unique style of soccer, one in a million.

*But what I discovered most in my time with
Wade, and what stood out most of all, he
had humbleness about him, where race or
color never mattered and that made him so
unique. That's why Wade stood out and was
special, and if I had learnt anything from
him, the one thing I learnt was to be humble.*

I will always miss him and love him.

Lemuel

Gosh! So, many wishes Lord, I can't take them all, "You cannot leave anything behind." Looking at all these wishes, and knowing that so many of us wish for the same thing, just standing here, not sure which way to go or what to do, looking left, then right, and at the wishes, then left again, afraid of which direction to choose, a piece of paper flies into my face. Pulling it from my face, I see my name on it. This is strange, my name, and as I start reading I'm amazed at what I see . . .

Hi Venessa,

*I decide to write you a letter telling you about
the impact Wade made in our lives. . . .*

*I sat watching this young little boy from the age of
eight years. What skill, always smiling and elated
about his performance on the soccer field. When
my son Joshua the same age started playing in the
same team, I looked at this young little boy, full
of life, chirpy beautiful green eyed boy and was
smitten. I wanted him to be a part of Josh's life
who, had just gone for surgery and was emotional.
I needed his positive energy. We started inviting*

him some weekends, not realizing that he would complete us and become a part of our family.

He became my eldest boy even though he was younger than Josh. He was just so much more mature than Josh. He was a role model to his brothers, because of their love for soccer. They learnt from him and we all learnt from each other. He was a breath of fresh air whenever he was around. Memories of our first holiday together, in September 2005. Boot Camp in Polokwane and at the crocodile farm then his 1st beach holiday to Durban, was home sick for you, but all too soon was having fun. That holiday was his first oysters, sushi and snails and did he love it. He loved my butternut soup and mussels in white sauce and when Demi joined I had to specially make for her as well. He also had a sweet tooth and was not shy at all to ask or tell me what to cook when he was around.

It's so amazing that I sense his presence when I'm in the kitchen or when we sitting at the dining room table sharing a meal where we would often have most of our chats. I want to share just a part of a message he wrote to me after I lost my mom 26/3/2011" Hey my mom . . . . No matter how far I am I am always alongside you in my heart remember that . . . I LOVE YOU ALWAYS . . . . This is what we all meant to each other.

Looking back I remember us laughing at when we attended mass he would say "aunty Dee you sing loud hey" and I would say do I sound false because he comes from a beautiful singing family. He would shyly lie (ha-ha) not to make me feel *bad and say "no, you sound good." I so remember how he knelt down to pray after he went up for his blessing, those praying hands. He was truly only here on borrowed time. His place was to be by His maker and in our hearts, forever and a day.*

Our son, Wade D Mulligan, our guardian angel up in heaven.

Deidre, Clint and his brothers.

Why this? Tears rolling, she's opened the box that I'm so desperately trying to get away from. "You say I need to see how Wade spread love, what good is that if it left behind only pain," angered at what I am left with . . .

Oh! Lord our daily prayer is to have Wade with us, but . . .

CHAPTER 9

THE REVELATION

. . . Is, that I will never get to catch the passing ball, that our wishes will never come true. I don't think we'll ever get over this, that the tears we shed for Wade will never turn into laughter, that dreams of such will never come true, that our prayers to have Wade with us will never be answered, that Wade is not coming back, and that life goes on, and that we have to find a way of living with all the questions.

The revelation is that you, the one question I noticed that would always surface when I opened the box, and would always be afloat, was exactly the same question, that was a constant thought which would keep popping up in my mind, Suddenly I see how you push your way through the waters pass all the other questions. I know you want me to look at you. I know that once again I'm in the box, and that I have to deal with you whether I like it or not. I guess I could never leave you behind and pretend you don't exist. I know you are wondering, why I left you all the time in the back of the memory box, because I was afraid that I would take you out of the box, and place you in the empty space in my heart. Knowing that you, the main question, was how Wade could take a permanent decision to a temporary situation, and in the process, almost destroy an entire family, if it was not for God's grace, a reminder of the disaster this question has left. It is because you are another one of questions that I would add to the open book, and would also walk with me. Wade, you were supposed to walk to me, but instead you chose to walk away. Not just away from me, but from your sisters, dads, grandfather, uncles, aunts, cousins, nephews, thousands of friends who are like brothers and colleagues. And once again, the realization of what life has handed me is there, and I'm so lost in a world where only pain exists. A sense of immense loss consumes my heart.

I'm wishing so, I could speak to you, to tell you to open my heart that you hold, so that I can let you see how my heart beats when I open that damn memory box, and the pain of that immense loss that consumes the heart.

Broken hearted I pick up all the wishes, closing my eyes, my last prayer as I start this journey, "Lord, grant us the faith, the grace, and the strength." Heart ripped open, the pain, stepping onto the road, the tears trickling down my cheeks forming a trail with each step, I stumble and fall, turning around to see what I've fallen over, shocked it's the memory box in the middle of the road, it's open. The reality of the open box is that it always will be where I am.

A glimPse into the box the . . .

THE FACEBOOK MESSAGE

. . . Rises to the surface. I'm at my desk going into the internet, suddenly, Wade's Facebook message pops up on my screen "Wade Mulligan would like to be your friend." How can this be? How could he want to be my friend on Facebook? I'm not on Facebook. The Facebook login comes up, without me doing anything. I enter his password and the information that comes up, scares the daylight out of me.

Facebook Login

Account Inaccessible

This account is in a special memorial state. If you have any questions or concerns, please visit the Help Center for further information.

Login as:

Wade Mulligan
<u>wademulligan@yahoo.com</u>
<u>Not Wade?</u>
Password:
Keep me logged in

Even Facebook knows, and has put his account in a special memorial state, and left me in one of my states again . . .

Don't do this, don't take me back please. A year has gone, but the cracks in my face reveal the pain of my life. But if you looked deeper, you'd see the million cracks in the heart. Take the heart, I can't bear the pain that comes from it, all because I forgot to close that darn box. I thought I left you. I thought we completed this Lord. So you a confirmation, that you will always remain open, never closed, or could never be left behind. Getting up, knees grazed and bleeding, I see in the distance the ball rolling down the road, running after the ball, I just have to pick it up. Don't want to leave anything behind, walking back to the box; I have to close you for now, flipping the lid close, picking it, up adding the wishes to the open book, holding them in my hands, lost and lonely . . .

I start my journey knowing that we cannot alter life, that life has no guarantee, and that I will never be able to live with this that I carry. The need for an encounter or vision, just like the thought of suicide, will probably linger and surface every now and then, whether I like it or not . . .

Where it will take me and my family, only God knows, but for now I know, that I have to continue on this journey . . .

I am aware that reading this book will open a lot of wounds, but through this, I hope that we will find peace in the process. Perhaps this will make a lot of children and parents realise, what the 'IMPACT OF A SUICIDE' leaves behind . . .

I hope that when reading this book, it will inspire you and make you realise that God, Jesus and Holy Spirit are real. That through the journey and suicide He was there for me and my family. With all the trials and tribulations, just remember that Jesus is walking with you and even if you decide to run ahead, just remember that He loves and prefers to have you beside Him. He will either run with you or you will stop, turn and walk back to Him or wait for Him. This is what I have discovered on this long road. I cannot run away from it or stay behind; I have to call out, reach out, and hold onto the only thing that makes sense in this entire ordeal.

I know that God has written this book through me . . .

"All parents are only disciples of Jesus, we can teach our children what God and Jesus have instilled in us, but what our children choose to learn from us is entirely up to them."

May God, Jesus and Holy Spirit bless you on your journey of life

Venessa.

A glimPse . . . "Remain Prayerful, Praise me and I will keep my Promise" . . .